CIVIL WAR GHOSTS OF
SOUTHWEST
MISSOURI

CIVIL WAR GHOSTS OF SOUTHWEST MISSOURI

LISA LIVINGSTON-MARTIN

Published by Haunted America
A Division of The History Press
Charleston, SC 29403
www.historypress.net

Front cover: Kendrick House, Carthage, Missouri. Built in 1849, it is one of the few prewar homes that survived destruction during the Civil War in southwest Missouri and is the site of unexplained phenomena. *Courtesy of L. Edward Martin.*

Back cover: Top: Union General Nathaniel Lyon, as depicted by *Harper's Weekly,* leading the charge at the Battle of Wilson's Creek, where he became the first general to die in battle during the Civil War. *Courtesy of Victorian Carthage, LLC, Kendrick House Collection.*

Bottom: The Battle of Carthage, July 5, 1861. *Gallant Attack of Major Siegel's Division on a Superior Force of Confederate Troops,* a colorized print from a sketch made at the scene, as it appeared in the *Pictorial War Record Magazine.* This was a glimpse of the violence to come for southwest Missouri. *Courtesy of Victorian Carthage, LLC, Kendrick House Collection.*

All images are by the author unless otherwise noted.

First published 2011
Manufactured in the United States

ISBN 978.1.60949.267.0

Library of Congress Cataloging-in-Publication Data
Livingston-Martin, Lisa.
Civil War ghosts of southwest Missouri / Lisa Livingston-Martin.
p. cm.

Includes bibliographical references.
ISBN 978-1-60949-267-0
1. Missouri--History--Civil War, 1861-1865. I. Title.
E517.L59 2011
977.8'03--dc22
2011016281

*For my parents, Homer Earl Livingston Jr. and Zola Marie Livingston.
All my love.*

CONTENTS

ACKNOWLEDGEMENTS

This project has been far from a solo effort. I am grateful to many people for supporting and helping me during this process. I thank my family for understanding and helping me in numerous ways, from tedious and mundane to fun and adventurous. My love and thanks to my amazing husband and three wonderful sons, mother and sisters who have put up with my distractions. Thank you to all of the Paranormal Science Lab team members, whose efforts make much of this project possible and who took on extra PSL duties while my time was limited:

Paranormal Science Lab:

Co-Team Leaders: Eric Crinnian, L. Edward Martin, Lisa Livingston-Martin and Brian Schwartz

Team Members: Jordyn Cole, Mistie Cole, Chelsea Copeland, Marla Anderson Copeland, Kelly Still Harris, Alex Martin, Bill Martin, Carla Martin and Lisa Still.

Thank you to those who have been supportive of Paranormal Science Lab and its efforts to bring attention to and to promote preservation efforts for Kendrick House in Carthage, Missouri. Thank you to Victorian Carthage, the nonprofit owner of Kendrick House, including Board of Directors members Kelly Still Harris, Bonnie Harris and Roberta Williams, who are more than caretakers of this wonderful historic home. Thank you to Mike Harris, John Hacker, Joe Hadsall, Kevin McClintock, Blake James, the *Carthage Press*, the *Joplin Globe*, *Joplin Metro Magazine*, *Show Me the Ozarks Magazine*, the *Joplin Fuse*, KOAM TV and the Missouri Humanities Council for spreading the word. Thank you to all of those who have attended PSL activities at Kendrick House, including the Haunted History Tours. We have made new friends and enjoyed sharing history and the paranormal with the public.

I am indebted to the knowledge of many people in researching and writing this book. I want to thank Steve Cottrell, author and expert on Civil War history in southwest Missouri, for insights. I also want to thank Steve Cottrell and Cliff Kester, who are both active in Civil War reenactments, for graciously posing for images that appear in this book, including appearing as our "ghostly" soldiers. I thank former and current property owners and residents of locations featured in *Civil War Ghosts of Southwest Missouri* for speaking with me. I learned many additional interesting facts during these conversations. In particular, thank you to Mr. and Mrs. Marston for their hospitality in sharing many details of their home, the historic antebellum Rothanbarger House, or "History House," in Joplin, Missouri. Thank you to

Paranormal Science Lab members at Fort Gibson, Oklahoma (Indian Territory), an important Union fort on the Fort Scott Military Road. *From left*: Brian Schwartz, Marla Anderson Copeland, Chelsea Copeland, L. Edward Martin, Lisa Livingston-Martin, Lisa Still and Mistie Cole. *Courtesy of Paranormal Science Lab, Jordyn Cole, photographer.*

the staff of the City of Carthage Civil War Museum; the Battle of Carthage Battlefield Park; the Bushwhacker Museum in Nevada, Missouri; Webb City Genealogy Society and Webb City Library, Webb City, Missouri; and the Baxter Springs Heritage Museum, Baxter Springs, Kansas.

Thank you to those who were kind enough to contribute use of your photographs: Paranormal Science Lab, Chelsea Copeland, Alex Martin, L. Edward Martin, Brian Schwartz and Victorian Carthage for use of items in the Kendrick House collection.

I wish to extend a special thank-you to Janice Tremeear, of Route 66 Paranormal Alliance of Springfield, Missouri, and author of *Missouri's Haunted Route 66: Ghosts Along the Mother Road* and the upcoming *Haunted Ozarks*, for encouragement and for the introduction to my editor, Ben Gibson. Thanks especially to Ben Gibson and everyone at The History Press for making this book a reality, a dream come true.

EMBERS ON THE
WESTERN WIND

PRECURSORS TO WAR IN SOUTHWEST MISSOURI

S outhwest Missouri was on one hand somewhat homogenous in that a large portion of the early settlers arrived from Southern states and a sense of the Southern culture was part of their daily lives. On the other hand, there was by no means a consensus of opinion as to the political issues of the time that ultimately embroiled this border area into the conflict.

The early settlers were a hardy group and self-reliant by nature and necessity. For the most part, they were industrious and prospered in the new land. Much of what we know of the earliest days of southwest Missouri comes from personal recollections, as many records were lost to fire during the Civil War. Many courthouses, commercial buildings, houses and farms were burned by one side or the other so that they could not be used as military positions and to make it more difficult for the opposing side to operate in the area. The characterization given by Judge J.A. Sturges, reflecting after many years on life in McDonald County, Missouri, in the 1850s, is typical of the region:

> *The people who had located here were generally from the south, more being from Tennessee than any other state, and had brought with them the manners and customs peculiar to those localities. They lived in primitive style, compared to the present, and were nearly self-sustaining. A cook stove was a rare exception, nearly every one cooking by the fireplace and oven...*

Many a delicious "pone," rare venison saddle and luscious [c]obbler has been cooked in this way…A sewing machine had never been heard of, while the clank of the loom and humming of the wheel furnished music almost as sweet, and more homelike than our present organs and pianos. The old fashioned linchpin wagons, with the box shaped like a canoe, many with wooden spindle, could be heard for miles as they groaned and creaked over the rocky roads. They raised their own cotton and wool, spun and wove it in the cloth and made their own garments. The latter was the women's work. Of course, every family cultivated enough tobacco for home consumption. Wheat and corn were produced and…there were a number of mills to do the grinding. Distilleries were quite numerous and manufactured the pure and unadulterated corn juice at twenty-five cents a gallon. The good people, both saints and sinners, could take their corn to the still and lay in a good supply of cash…In this new country subject to chills and malaria, and the scarcity of doctors and drugs, no doubt this pure liquor drove disease and death from many a home. Hogs and cattle could be raised with very little feed…while deer, turkey and other game were found in abundance. One man told me that his father said his store bill before the war did not average more than five dollars a year. His family was quite large, and they lived comfortably. Instead of doing without, they simply produced what was required…Many families…had well furnished houses, and gold watches and jewelry were worn quite extensively. Several parties owned slaves and carried on quite extensive plantations. Almost any McDonald county farmer, along in the fifties could raise a hundred dollars any day, and real estate mortgages were unknown. People were honest in their dealings and paid their debts, and the latch string to every cabin hung on the outside. People were hospitable, extremely so. Partly because it was born and bred in them, partly because, being isolated, and the settlements scarce and far between, it was regarded as a treat to have a neighbor or stranger stop to dinner or overnight. But the question is asked, how did they make any money?…A farmer could gather up his hogs and cattle in the spring after the grass was good, and drive them to St. Louis. There was range all the way and it mattered little that it took a long time to make the journey. What his produce brought was clear profit. He frequently returned with several hundred dollars. Horses were raised and taken directly to the southern market where they would bring from $75 to $100. Thus an industrious man could soon acquire quite a snug sum of money.

A typical log cabin home found in southwest Missouri in the Civil War period. *Courtesy of L. Edward Martin.*

The early settlers were not as much alike regarding politics, especially with regard to the coming war. They fell into three categories generally. There were unconditional Union men, who supported the Union at any cost, even after declaration of war. A second group, conditional Union men, was composed of both Union supporters and Southern sympathizers who believed in supporting the Federal government as long as the Union did not fight to force the secessionist states back into the Union. The third group, called secessionists, was composed of Southern sympathizers who advocated that Missouri secede from the Union even if by force. It was not unusual for members of the same family to take different positions or to fight on opposite sides once war was declared. That said, many tried to remain neutral, especially as the level of violence escalated. While many foresaw the coming war, it is not as clear how many predicted the nature of the conflict that would be waged in their backyards. Some also lost their initial enthusiasm for the cause as loss of life and property continued for four long years.

The Border War was a crucible along the border of Missouri and Kansas, most bitter along the southern part of the border, even years before the outbreak of formal hostilities. Why here instead of the Mason-Dixon line in the East? The Missouri Compromise, which allowed Missouri to enter the Union as a slave state but limited slavery in the future to south of the line along the southern border of Missouri, was an attempt to keep the balance between Southern and Northern states in Congress. Subsequently, more strained and contorted compromises allowed entry of other states into the Union. For instance, the Compromise of 1850, among other things, allowed California into the Union as a free state, resulting in a majority in Congress for Northern states. In 1854, it was apparent that Kansas and Nebraska would become states. The influential Illinois Democratic senator Stephen Douglas, political rival of Abraham Lincoln, engineered a solution that on first impression seemed rational. Kansas and Nebraska were allowed to enter the Union and determine their own stance on the issue of slavery. However, Douglas had personal interest in ensuring the compromise was passed. He had a stake in the transcontinental railroad then being built, and he desired that the eastern hub be Chicago, in his home state. Nebraska was not suitable to slavery due to climate and landscape and its location along the northern emigration route, meaning it would be settled by Northerners, so that the ultimate route of the transcontinental railroad would safely be placed in Northern territory. Although Kansas was never realistically a good candidate for widespread slave labor, it was along the same emigration route from the Southern states as was southern Missouri. Kansas became the symbolic battleground over the future of slavery. An unintended consequence to this solution to the Kansas-Nebraska slavery issue was a clash of Northern and Southern culture along the Missouri-Kansas border, which would have great impact on the region in the coming war.

Abolitionists in New England set out to ensure that Northerners settled Kansas, and established companies, such as the New England Company, designed to solicit settlers for Kansas by the use of propaganda. This policy ignored the fact that there were a large number of people already living in the Kansas territory, including people who had held slaves in Kansas lawfully under federal law for many years. Many Missourians had made land claims in the Kansas territory. The new arrivals ignored the existing legal claims of landowners where the preexisting owner was a Southern sympathizer or owned slaves. As such, tensions mounted quickly. Soon, residents across the border in Missouri were living along an open border with settlements of "radical" abolitionists who were willing to impose their views upon those around them, increasingly with extreme means, including raids into

Missouri to liberate slaves, burn homes and commit murder. As the dispute over slavery spilled out of Kansas and affected Missourians directly, border retaliation soon followed. Most of the slave population in Missouri was along the Mississippi River to the east and north of the Missouri River in northern Missouri. Despite that fact, the most intense border violence in this prewar period came out of Linn County, Kansas, in the form of raids into Bates and Vernon Counties in southwest Missouri. Federal law and Kansas territorial law each protected the proslavery settlers as well as the interests of Missouri residents whose slaves had been taken by abolitionists. The Federal government tried to enforce legal rights of the citizens, which in the eyes of many abolitionists meant that the Federal army was proslavery, leading to clashes. Federal troops enforcing the rights of the proslavery settlers in Kansas included a number of men who played key roles in the war in Missouri, including the future Confederate general Joseph Shelby and army scouts Buffalo Bill Cody and Wild Bill Hickok. A symbolic illustration of the change to come is the fact that the abolitionist newcomers started raiding army posts in Kansas. In one raid during 1856, they captured a brass cannon from the Mexican War named "Old Sacramento" that, five years later, would be used by the Federal army, commanded by Colonel Franz Sigel, against the Missouri State Militia and Confederate forces at the first major land battle of the Civil War: the Battle of Carthage, in southwest Missouri.

After the election of Abraham Lincoln as president in 1860, the outgoing Missouri governor, Robert Stewart, in his last gubernatorial speech, echoed the majority opinion of Missourians, noting that Missouri had even by then suffered great violence as a result of the fighting in Kansas and that some western counties were almost depopulated. His labels of depredations committed, including murder, arson and theft at the hands of "bandit hordes" of abolitionists, would be used by Union activists in Missouri a short time later regarding Confederate supporters, with each side's rhetoric using interchangeable terms. Stewart further voiced the majority opinion that Missouri should remain in the Union if possible and that armed neutrality was preferable to secession. He expressed loyalty to his state first but only slightly more than to the Union:

> *Missouri occupies a position to those troubles that should make her voice potent in the councils of the nation. With scarcely a disunionist per se to be found in her borders, she is still determined to demand, and to maintain*

her rights at every hazard. She loves the Union while it is the protector of equal rights, but will despise it as the instrument of wrong. She came into the Union upon a compromise, and is willing to abide by a fair compromise still…Missouri has a right to speak on this subject because she has suffered. Bounded on three sides by free territory her border counties have been the frequent scenes of kidnapping and violence, and this State has probably lost as much, in the last two years, in the abduction of slaves, as all of the rest of the Southern States. At this moment some of the western counties are desolated, and almost depopulated, from the fear of a bandit horde, who have been committing depredations—arson, theft and foul and murder—upon the adjacent border…As matters are at present, Missouri will stand by her lot, and hold to the Union as long it is worth an effort to preserve it. So long as there is hope of success she will seek for justice within the Union. She cannot be frightened from her propriety by the past unfriendly legislation of the North, nor be dragooned into secession by the extreme South. If those who should be our friends and allies, undertake to render our property worthless by a system of prohibitory laws, or by reopening the slave trade in opposition to the moral sense of the civilized world, and at the same time reduce us to the position of an humble sentinel to watch over and protect their interests, receiving all of the blows and none of the benefits, Missouri will hesitate long before sanctioning such an arrangement. She will rather take the high position of armed neutrality. She is able to take care of herself, and will be neither forced nor flattered, driven nor coaxed, into a course of action that must end in her own destruction. If South Carolina and other Cotton States, persist in secession, she will desire to see them go in peace, with the hope that a short experience at separate government, and an honorable readjustment of the Federal compact, will induce them to return to their former position… Whilst I would recommend the adoption of all proper measures and influences to secure the just acknowledgement and protection of our rights, and in the final failure of this, a resort to the last painful remedy of separation; yet, regarding as I do, the American Confederacy as the source of a thousand blessings, pecuniary, social, and moral, and its destruction as fraught with incalculable loss, suffering, and crime, I would here, in my last public official act as Governor of Missouri, record my solemn protest against unwise and hasty action, and my unalterable devotion to the Union so long as it can be made the protector of equal rights.

Georgia City, three miles from Kansas, was the scene of repeated raids by Kansas Jayhawkers, who resorted to murder and arson in Missouri during prewar days. The cemetery is the only evidence that a town once stood in these fields. *Courtesy of the author.*

Governor Claiborne Jackson's inaugural speech was much different—and less flexible. His statements demonstrated a loyalty to the Union last, to Missouri second and to the extremist Southern views of the Southern states of his boyhood first. Jackson, commenting upon the growing abolitionist movement, stated:

> *The prominent characteristic of this party…is that it is purely sectional in its loyalty and its principles. The only principle inscribed upon its banner is* Hostility to Slavery;…*its object not merely to confine slavery within its present limits; not merely to exclude it from the Territories, and prevent the formation and admission of any slave-holding States; not merely to abolish it in the District of Columbia, and interdict its passage from one State to another, but to strike down its existence everywhere; to sap its foundation in public sentiment; to annoy and harass, and gradually destroy its vitality, by every means, direct, or indirect, physical and moral, which human ingenuity can devise. The triumph of such an organization is not the victory of a political party, but the domination of a Section. It proclaims in significant*

tones the destruction of the equality among the States which is the vital cement of our federal Union…Accordingly, we find the result of the most recent Presidential election [Abraham Lincoln becoming president] *has already produced its natural effects* [South Carolina's secession from the Union]. *From Florida to Missouri a feeling of discontent and alarm has manifested itself, more or less violent, according to the imminence of the danger, and the extent of the interest at stake. The cotton-growing States, have a larger and more vital interest in jeopardy than the Border Wars, and are the first to awaken to a sense of insecurity. The sagacious Southern statesman is fully aware that his section, although necessarily the last victim, will be the greatest sufferer; that when the outposts yield, the citadel will not long afford safety. With them the alternative is the maintenance of that institution which Great Britain forced upon their ancestors* [taxation without representation], *or the conversion of their homes into desert wastes…It has been said to be quite easy to bear the calamities of our neighbors with philosophical equanimity. Let us not illustrate this maxim by criticizing the precipitancy of the South. They are not the aggressors. They only ask to be let alone. If some have regarded their action as hasty, has not the occasion been extraordinary? I do not stand here to justify or to condemn the action of South Carolina in withdrawing her allegiance to the Federal Government…If South Carolina has acted hastily, let not her error lead to the more fatal one—an attempt at coercion. The destiny of the slave-holding States of this Union is one and the same…And Missouri will in my opinion best consult her own interests, and the interests of the whole country, by a timely declaration of her determination to stand by her sister slave-holding States, in whose wrongs she participates, and with whose institutions and people she sympathizes…So far as Missouri is concerned, her citizens have ever been devoted to the Union, and she will remain in it so long as there is any hope that it will maintain the spirit and guarantees of the Constitution.*

The change in position of the Federal government, as to whose interests would be championed upon secession of the Southern states in 1861, undoubtedly played a role in the decisions to be made by Governor Jackson over the following months. It also affected the decision of many Federal military officers on the western border to join the Confederate army. The hope, given at least lip service by Governor Jackson, of remaining loyal to the Federal government was quickly cast aside. Shortly after this inaugural address, the Missouri State Guard was assembled near the federal arsenal in St. Louis. Although peaceful intentions were expressed, this act was viewed by Federal army officers as a prelude to seizing the federal arsenal in St. Louis. After the fall of Fort Sumter, President Lincoln called on governors to raise seventy-five thousand men, with Missouri's quota being four regiments. Governor Jackson's response was to declare that the request of the president was illegal, unconstitutional and revolutionary. Jackson also ordered the U.S. arsenal in Liberty, near Kansas City, seized on April 20, 1861. The Missouri State Guard was encamped at Camp Jackson, not far from the capitol at Jefferson City, in central Missouri, and Jackson brazenly named streets in Camp Jackson after Confederate leaders, such as "Davis" and "Beauregard." Captain Nathaniel Lyon was in charge of the U.S. arsenal in St. Louis and was concerned about these events. Rumors were that munitions from federal arsenals were being hauled into Camp Jackson. Lyon decided to assess the situation personally. He disguised himself in a dress, shawl and bonnet and, accompanied by Captain J.J. Witzig, rode in a carriage through Camp Jackson undetected. His observations led him to take action.

The Missouri State Guard Flag was used by Governor Claiborne Jackson's forces at Camp Jackson and during the march into southwest Missouri, including the Battle of Carthage. This example appears in the collection of the City of Carthage Civil War Museum. *Courtesy of the author.*

A Union Safety Committee in St. Louis had been authorized by President Lincoln and the secretary of war to quietly raise men for defense of the city in case of attack. This allowed Union supporters to raise an army for use by Captain Lyon while letting the Rebels believe there were only a small number of soldiers in St. Louis to defend the arsenal. In mission, it served the same function as the partisan ranger and guerrilla units would after war was declared. Lyon gained approval from the Safety Committee to take preemptive action to seize Camp Jackson before Jackson's Missouri State Guard attacked more federal installations, especially the St. Louis arsenal. Word of Lyon's plan reached General Frost of the Missouri State Guard, who replied by sending a letter of assurance that no hostile acts were intended. Lyon replied that Frost's command of the Missouri State Guard was viewed as hostile toward the federal government; that he knew Frost was in direct communication with the Confederacy and receiving supplies from it; and that the refusal to disperse the Missouri State Guard was disobedience of the president's proclamation. He demanded the immediate surrender of Frost and the Missouri State Guard, promising that the prisoners would be humanely and kindly treated. While the message was clear, Lyon had already left St. Louis with six to seven thousand well-armed troops and twenty pieces of artillery before the letter reached Frost.

On May 10, 1861, Lyon surrounded Camp Jackson. Hundreds of people, some armed, including women and children, gathered to watch what transpired. Lyon demanded Frost's surrender. Frost, after consulting with his officers and staff, determined that resistance was unrealistic and complied. The Missouri State Guard troops were taken prisoner but were offered release upon condition that they take an oath to support the U.S. Constitution and to not take up arms against the Federal government. Only eight or ten men took the oath, the rest preferring confinement. About eight hundred prisoners were marched in line toward St. Louis, enclosed on either side by U.S. soldiers. When a halt was made, large numbers of civilians would press forward, jeering. Some German American soldiers at the front of the line lost patience and opened fire. No injuries resulted, and the soldiers who had opened fire were placed under arrest. Then multiple volleys were heard from the rear of the line, and civilians, including women and children, were seen fleeing and were fired upon, with about twenty-five killed or wounded, including two women and a child. The soldiers who fired claimed that they had been attacked by the crowd with stones and fired at the command of

Troops marched through southwest Missouri, often on "roads" that were little more than animal trails. Reenactment photo. *Courtesy of L. Edward Martin.*

an officer. A regiment of German American Federal soldiers took control of Camp Jackson, and there was much agitation on the part of civilians.

U.S. General Harney, Lyon's commanding officer, approved of Lyon's actions but issued a proclamation intended to calm emotions. Two days later, the state legislature passed what was called the Military Bill, which authorized the arming of the militia. General Harney issued another proclamation declaring the Military Bill an indirect secession ordinance that ignored the protocols used by other states that had formally seceded; he stated that it was unconstitutional and void. However, he declared that he did not intend to use the soldiers in his command unless forced to do so. Under the Military Bill, Governor Jackson placed General Sterling Price in command of the Missouri State Guard. Price and Harney met in St. Louis on May 21, 1861, and signed an agreement by which management of the Missouri State Guard was turned over to Price, under Jackson's supervision. Harney declared that he had no intention of military movement that would otherwise "create excitement and jealousies." Harney issued a proclamation to the people of Missouri that the forces of the state and the Federal government were both pledged to bring about peace. Harney had signed the agreement with Price and issued the proclamation for peace without authority of the Federal government, and he was relieved of his command. In fact, Harney had already taken steps to remove Federal troops from the state of Missouri. Lyon replaced Harney in command. In the meantime, Jackson and Price, pursuant to the agreement, disbanded the state troops at Jefferson City and ordered them to go home.

The removal of Harney and replacement by Lyon hastened the confrontation that soon erupted in southwest Missouri. While it seems apparent that Governor Jackson was headed down the road to secession, but for this twist of events, General Price may well have remained a Union man, as he had been vocally opposed to secession. By his own statements, it was due to his loyalty to Missouri that he felt compelled to join the Confederate army. A second conference was held in St. Louis on June 11, 1861, in an attempt to reconcile the state and Federal positions. Lyon, newly promoted to the rank of general, was accompanied by Colonel Francis Blair and Major H.A. Conant. The state was represented by Governor Jackson, General Price and Colonel Thomas Snead. Jackson wanted to avoid the Federal government ordering enlistment of men to force the Confederate States back into the Union and advocated for a compromise, wanting both governments to agree to not recruit troops within Missouri. An eyewitness to the negotiations reported Lyon's response as:

> Shaking his head, Lyon rose and in his measured, even, earnest tones said, "Rather than agree that my government shall concede to your government one iota of authority as to one man to be recruited, one inch of soil to be divided in allegiance or neutralized between my government and your government, I will see you, Sir (pointing to Price), and you, Sir (pointing to Jackson), and myself, and all of us, under the sod!" Then taking out his watch he glanced at it, and added: "You shall have safe conduct out of my lines for one hour. Meanwhile, you can get dinner. It is now three o'clock."

Hurriedly dining, Jackson, Price and Snead took an express train out of St. Louis. Fearing that Lyon would pursue them to Jefferson City, they burned bridges and cut telegraph lines behind them. The next day, Jackson called into active service fifty thousand militiamen, "for the purpose of repelling invasion, and for the protection of the lives, liberty and property of the citizens of the State." Lyon likewise responded one day after Jackson's activation of the militia by heading up the Missouri River on steamboats.

The Missouri State Guard and the State Militia were composed of citizens who normally would be tending their farms or other routine work. Reenactment photo. *Courtesy of L. Edward Martin.*

Upon hearing of Lyon's approach, Governor Jackson and General Price left the capital on the steamboat *White Cloud*. On June 15, 1861, Lyon arrived at Jefferson City and took control of the city. With Jackson gone, the state was without a chief executive until June 30, 1861, when the state convention met and named Hamilton Gamble to replace Jackson.

By June 16, 1861, Jackson and Price were at Boonville with three to four thousand men men. Lyon, having left men to secure Jefferson City, arrived in Boonville. General Price had taken seriously ill and left Boonville by steamboat to go to his home in Chariton County to recuperate. Governor Jackson, with Colonel Marmaduke, was left to face Lyon. The forces met near Boonville, and Lyon opened with several rounds of artillery. Jackson's men were poorly armed and not disciplined. The state troops behaved bravely in face of the artillery but were eventually forced into retreat. Lyon had two men killed, nine wounded and one missing. Jackson had two men killed and several wounded. This was a small skirmish but the first of many in Missouri. By the end of 1861, Missouri was the scene of nearly half of the casualties and half of the incidents of combat of the war to that time.

The National Cemetery No. 2, north of the site of Union Fort Blair, is an unexpected sight on the rolling prairie. Many Civil War soldiers from southwest Missouri and southeast Kansas are interred here. *Courtesy of L. Edward Martin.*

Jackson was now in essence a Confederate government in exile. With the loss of the capital and Camp Jackson, he turned south, hoping to enlist support from the regular Confederate army in Arkansas. This decision brought the war to southwest Missouri. As for the exile government, Jackson ultimately called a Secession Convention at the Masonic Lodge in Neosho, Newton County, Missouri, in the extreme southwest corner of the state. The convention voted to secede from the Union on October 21, 1861, and Neosho became the site of the "Confederate Capitol" of Missouri, although Jackson spent much of the rest of the war outside of Missouri before dying of cancer in Little Rock, Arkansas, on December 6, 1862. The journey to a Secession Convention and a Confederate government in exile was not played out upon distant battlefields reported in newspapers weeks afterward but in the tilled fields, homes and streets of southwest Missouri, which had already become before the outbreak of war, in former Governor Stewart's words, "desolated, and almost depopulated, from the fear of a bandit horde."

During the course of the Civil War, more than 1,150 battles and skirmishes were fought in Missouri, or 11 percent of the war's total, with more occurring in Missouri during 1861 than in any other state and more occurring in Missouri during the entire war than all other states except Virginia and Tennessee. More than 40,000 Missourians served in the Confederate army, and more than 110,000 served in the Union army. Additionally, thousands served as partisan rangers or guerrillas with authorized mandates from one army or the other.

THE TORCH IS LIT

WAR COMES TO SOUTHWEST MISSOURI

The first Confederate flag (the official Stars and Bars) to be flown in Missouri was in southwest Missouri on a makeshift flagpole on the Sarcoxie square in April 1861. Before the armies fired the first shots in southwest Missouri, there were calls for secession, such as Judge Chenault in Jasper County, who in May 1861 delivered public speeches on the square in Carthage, Missouri, in favor of secession, with the Stars and Bars flying from the flagpole on the courthouse yard. Other secession calls came from the local press and businessmen such C.C Dawson, publisher of the *Southwest News*, of Carthage, Missouri, and Thomas R. Livingston, a prominent miner and businessman who also owned smelters, mills and a trading post, with operations at Minersville (now Oronogo), Granby, French Point and Indian Territory (Oklahoma). Livingston raised and drilled a militia in preparation for the inevitable fighting to come. Livingston was known to be good-natured but capable of beating five or six men in a fight. Although a secessionist, he was typical of many slaveholders in the area, owning one slave. Answering Governor Jackson's call, Livingston and many other men of southwest Missouri enlisted in the initial ninety-day enlistment of the Missouri State Guard. Upon its expiration, Livingston received a command as a Confederate partisan ranger and raised a regiment of men in Jasper County, Missouri, the First Missouri Cavalry Battalion, First Indian Brigade, "Cherokee Spikes," also known as the "Bloody Spikes."

Cavalry was a necessity in the rolling hills and prairies of southwest Missouri. Expert horsemen on good horses enabled Confederate guerrilla units to interrupt Union troop and supply movements throughout the war. Reenactment photo. *Courtesy of L. Edward Martin.*

The rest of southwest Missouri was similarly faced with political and loyalty tension as displayed in Carthage and Neosho. The eastern side of southwest Missouri was no less contentious in June 1861. West Plains, in Howell County, had only been in existence about four years but had grown into a social and commercial center for the county. County business ground to a halt when Circuit Judge James McBride, who had been made Confederate Brigadier General McBride, feared that Federal troops at Rolla would come after him. He ordered that Howell County men who would not take an oath of allegiance to the Confederacy be hanged, despite the fact that Missouri had not seceded from the Union. Judge McBride and the county sheriff led a large group of men tracking down their Union-supporting neighbors. Many Union men joined the Confederate cause out of fear.

Various labels have been used to describe the irregular units and unofficial bands of men roaming southwestern Missouri during the Civil War. Generally, those groups can be divided as follows: units raised with consent and acquiescence of the Union and Confederate armies are referred to as partisan rangers and guerrillas because they used guerrilla warfare as their principal means of pursuing the interests of the army for which they were operating. The term bushwhacker was applied to these groups as well when discussing a group with opposite loyalties to the speaker; the term bushwhacker also applied to groups of men who had no military or political allegiance but who used the war as an opportunity to pursue plunder, theft and violence in the region, which was a vacuum without effective law enforcement.

THE BATTLE OF CARTHAGE

On July 5, 1861, some sixteen days prior to Bull Run, the North and South were clashing in southwest Missouri at the Battle of Carthage. The day before, July 4, Colonel Franz Sigel and his troops were in Carthage, and many civilians were nervous to see the German American soldiers, referred to as "the Dutch." Sigel walked the streets speaking with citizens trying to calm fears and tensions. Some soldiers walked to the square, where they were greeted by, among others, Union supporters, including the teenage daughters of the former sheriff, Norris Hood. The Hood girls unfurled a Stars and Stripes flag at the approach of the soldiers. That night, Sigel camped at James Spring, on the east side of present-day Carthage, and on the bluff above the spring that overlooked the trail to Sarcoxie, to the east. On the bluff stood the home of Elwood and Elizabeth (Richardson) James, for whom the spring was named. Although the Jameses were from Virginia, a slaveholding state, they were far from Southern sympathizers. They moved and built a home on this picturesque bluff in 1842, when Elwood was elected the first county clerk/circuit clerk and recorder of deeds of Jasper County. He also relocated his mercantile business from the first county seat of Sarcoxie to the new county seat at Carthage. During the 1850s and 1860s, members of the James family were active in the Underground Railroad movement, and the house and a cave above the spring were utilized as hiding places for runaway slaves on their way to freedom. Local lore holds that the cave was connected to the house by a tunnel, although no evidence to verify this legend has come to light and such a tunnel would have been several hundred feet in length and would have been dug through a hillside composed of red clay and rocks. The entrance to the cave is now partially collapsed, and based upon observation, it appears doubtful that a tunnel could have been dug out in secret with sufficient supports to prevent cave-ins and also remain invisible to casual passersby, which would have been absolutely necessary for safety. It seems more likely that there were separate hiding spaces in the cave and house. One of Elizabeth James's family members was John Richardson, who, at the outbreak of the war, was the publisher of a newspaper in Springfield and one of the few in southwest Missouri who supported Abraham Lincoln in the presidential election of 1860. By the summer of 1861, he was a civilian aide to Colonel Franz Sigel in the U.S. Army Volunteers and was Sigel's primary guide on July 5, 1861, at the Battle of Carthage.

The spring is now known as Carter Spring for Dr. John A. Carter, who during the Reconstruction period built a large brick mansion on the foundation of

The entrance to the Battle of Carthage State Historic Site and Park. This is the location where Franz Sigel and his men camped the night of July 4, 1861, on the eve of the battle. On the night of July 5, the Confederate forces under Governor Claiborne Jackson and General McCullough camped on this same site. *Courtesy of Paranormal Science Lab, Alex Martin, photographer.*

James Spring (now Carter Spring) at the Battle of Carthage State Historic Site and Park. In the background, on the right, is the entrance to the cave used as a hiding place for runaway slaves on the Underground Railroad. *Courtesy of Paranormal Science Lab, Alex Martin, photographer.*

the original James house. The Carter House still stands watch atop the bluff and is still used as a private residence. It also housed the first radio station in the Carthage area (KDMO) and, consequently, was called the "Radio House" in the past. I have heard accounts from people who have visited the Carter House, which sits behind a tall, ornate iron fence and gates, that they consider it to be haunted, with feelings of being watched and odd noises.

On the morning of July 5, Sigel marched north of town, and the two forces met north of Dry Fork, some eight miles north of town. Originally, General Lyon and Sigel planned on meeting and trapping Jackson's forces in a pincher maneuver, but Lyon was still more than one hundred miles north, and Sigel was vastly outnumbered by Jackson's Missouri State Guard and the regular Confederate forces under General McCullough out of Arkansas. Governor Jackson oversaw the opening shots of the battle, becoming the only sitting governor to lead troops into battle during the Civil War, although this was short-lived, as once the battle intensified, Jackson relinquished field command to General Rains. The battle began with exchanges of artillery. Jackson maneuvered to surround Sigel's smaller army, but Sigel saw the flanking maneuver and opted to retreat rather than attack and be cut off and surrounded.

The fighting turned back toward Carthage, crossing Buck Branch, then on past the Kendrick House and forded Spring River before reaching the streets of Carthage. There was fighting in the streets, and civilians were drawn into the animosities. The battle turned to urban guerrilla tactics as it became a house-to-house fight. Among those civilians witnessing the fighting was fourteen-year-old Myra Belle Shirley, later famous as Belle Starr, who helped nurse wounded in the streets. The Shirley family, Southern sympathizers and slaveholders, had multiple tracts of land in Jasper County. Myra's father, John Shirley, owned the Shirley Hotel and tavern on the north side of the square. None of those prewar buildings survived the war due to the town being burned multiple times. A plaque in the sidewalk commemorates the spot where the hotel was located. This was Myra's first brush with the violence of war, but not her last. Her older brother, Bud, joined the Confederate cause, fighting with bushwhackers, only to be shot while eating supper at a house in nearby Sarcoxie about a year after the Battle of Carthage. The family retrieved his body and buried him secretly. Some say that he was buried at the old City Cemetery in Carthage, where Central Park is now. Most of the graves were moved to make way for the park, and those of soldiers killed in the Civil War were reinterred at the National Cemetery in Springfield, Missouri. However, it is known that not all of the graves were moved, as later, when digging to make way for improvements, graves were unearthed. There are other stories of Bud being buried in various locations under cover of darkness out of fear that enemies would desecrate the body. The Shirley family gave up their home and business and headed to Texas during the war, as did many other Southern sympathizers in southwest Missouri. Some speculate that Bud's body was dug up and his body taken to Texas with the family to be reinterred. Central Park has had sightings of ghostly figures over the years that are thought to be those whose graves were not properly moved and victims of the war. Whether Bud Shirley is among those apparitions is an unanswered question.

The fighting proceeded to the southeast side of town, and a final intense skirmish ensued for two and a half hours in the evening. While Sigel's more disciplined, experienced troops retreated east to Sarcoxie that night, Jackson, Rains and McCullough allowed a vastly smaller force to escape with few casualties. Sigel's use of the artillery prevented a more serious defeat. One

The Battle of Carthage, Missouri—Gallant Attack of Major Siegel's Division on a Superior Force of Confederate Troops, a colorized print from a sketch made at the scene, as it appeared in the *Pictorial War Record Magazine. Courtesy of Victorian Carthage, LLC, Kendrick House collection.*

of the Union cannons was lost fording one of the various rivers that day and was thought to be on an island in the middle of Spring River. The cannon has never been found, despite many earnest searchers' best efforts. However, river channels have changed course over the intervening 150 years and it may have been lost at one of the other crossings. It is one remaining mystery yet to be solved. The Confederate force camped at James Spring that night, the same site where Sigel had spent the previous night, and would have collected water from the spring within sight of the cave used in the Underground Railroad.

In terms of losses, the Federals had thirteen killed and thirty-one wounded, and the Confederates had twelve killed, sixty-four wounded and one missing. The Federal army retreated to Mount Vernon and then to Springfield, where Sigel waited for General Lyon's arrival with much-needed reinforcements. The Confederate army took control of Carthage and areas south, including garrisons at Neosho, Granby and Newtonia.

There were prisoners taken on both sides. There were no facilities or practical means of keeping prisoners, particularly at this early juncture in the war. The experience of a unit of Federal soldiers illustrates the heated emotions that were already affecting the region. The young commanding officer was in charge of a unit of German Americans. They were taken prisoner by Jackson's men, and as they were marched through Carthage, insults were yelled and ladies of the town walked up to the soldiers and spit in their faces, although the soldiers had made no remarks or other behavior to provoke such an insult. The openly hostile treatment did not end at the edge of Carthage. The prisoners were marched to Neosho, some fifteen miles south, where McCullough was garrisoned. At that point, Jackson threatened to have the "damned Dutch" prisoners shot. The Federal soldiers later recounted that General McCullough, who was a regular Confederate officer, unlike Jackson, told Jackson that should Jackson or his men harm the prisoners he would turn his guns on them instead. The prisoners related that they were treated well by the regular Confederate troops but could not say the same for Jackson's Missouri State Guard. As quickly became the practice, the prisoners were shortly paroled to walk to Springfield, some sixty miles away, and rejoin their command. The citizens of Neosho threatened to kill the prisoners. Their hostility was enough that General McCullough provided a military escort out of Neosho for the paroled soldiers for their safety.

With the retreat of the Union army, the publisher of the Carthage newspaper, the *Southwest News*, closed the office and took the printing press to McDonald County, where he put the press to work printing money for Jackson's secessionist state government. This money was printed on paper torn from records books of the Jasper County Circuit Clerk's Office. Businesses in Carthage were abandoned, merchandise still on store shelves. Thus began the transformation of southwest Missouri into a burnt wasteland, and by war's end, the transformation was complete.

As the war progressed, guerrilla attacks, intentional fires set by both sides and neglect allowed the area to decay back into the wilderness. Carthage was burned to the ground in 1863, with witnesses describing the swirling smoke as appearing like a circling wagon train. Virtually all structures were destroyed. The two-story brick courthouse that became a battered shell was used by both armies and guerrillas periodically, as it gave a vantage point for miles. One Union soldier described Carthage in the later days of the war, saying that the stench of death was smelled before they reached town. There were so few people remaining that corpses lay on the ground where they fell from gunshots. A scene is described of camping on the square and a soldier inadvertently standing so that the heel of his boot was in the hollow of a human jawbone, appearing almost as a spur, causing the diarist to shudder at the comparison raised in his mind. Firsthand accounts were summed up in *An Illustrated Historical Atlas of Jasper County, Missouri* in 1876:

> *Only five dwellings had escaped destruction. Ruins made the place unsightly. The old chimneys became the nests of owls, which hooted gloomily and forebodily over the silent and desolate scene. The deserted public square and streets, overgrown with weeds, were given up to wolves and deer, except when wandering bands of marauders, the only human visitors, would stop to feed their horses and then mount and ride away.*

This fate was not isolated through the region. One Union scout riding through Dade County, near Greenfield, reported that one could ride forty to fifty miles without seeing a living person. The land was so barren, with farmsteads and crops burned or fallow, that he requested permission to leave southwest Missouri, as there was not enough forage to feed the horses.

Ghostly soldiers in Civil War uniforms are said to have been seen on the square, on the courthouse yard and nearby. If there were to be ghosts of soldiers in Carthage, this is a likely place, although I have never encountered one there. The current courthouse was built in 1894 and is an imposing three-story stone building with taller towers, inaccessible to the public, reminiscent of fortifications. Perhaps the effect was not entirely accidental.

The Battle of Carthage Battlefield Park includes Carter Spring, known at the time of the war as James Spring. There are various types of paranormal activity experienced at the park. This site will be discussed in more detail in the sections on paranormal investigation. Likewise, Kendrick House, one of three prewar homes reputedly not destroyed in the war, was occupied by both armies at various times and was the scene of guerrilla violence. The Kendrick family lived in the home for more than 130 years. The house is now owned by Victorian Carthage, a nonprofit group that preserves Kendrick House as a living museum. Paranormal Science Lab has conducted extensive paranormal investigations onsite, and paranormal activity at Kendrick House will be discussed in detail in the sections on paranormal investigation.

WARTIME EXPERIENCES IN
THE WEST PLAINS AREA

As Governor Jackson was marching his men toward southwest Missouri, like-minded men were rallying across the region. On July 1, 1861, in West Plains, there was a Confederate rally, with a speakers' stand and seating for several hundred people built just east of Town Spring. The Stars and Bars, the official Confederate flag, was raised for the first time in Howell County. Union men raised the Stars and Stripes on either side of the speakers' area, and each side rallied around its flag. Speakers came to town from various southwest Missouri locations, including Judge "Wild Bill" Price of Springfield. Tensions were high, and warnings were made for Union men to remain silent or be shot full of holes. During a lull, William Monks walked to the speakers' stand and announced there would be a Union meeting at Black's store the following Saturday, July 6, 1861. He then invited people to come and hear Union speeches and the reading of the Constitution while the Confederate rally continued. Men stood rifles in hand, and each side demanded the other lower its flag. Finally, it was agreed that both sides would lower their flags at the same time, and violence was averted. Three Confederate units were raised that day. No Union units were ever raised in Howell County.

As promised, the following Saturday, July 6, 1861, the Union meeting was held and speeches made. The Confederates had announced that Union men would be arrested or pressed into service of the Confederate army, and their leaders were to be hanged. Monks wisely decided to not go directly home

Lisa Livingston-Martin stands next to a six-inch Confederate cannon in the collection of the Baxter Springs Heritage Museum, Baxter Springs, Kansas. *Courtesy of L. Edward Martin.*

after the meeting. The following day, at 11:00 p.m., twenty-five Confederate men rode to the farm of William Monks, including nine men who were personal acquaintances and friends of Monks. Monks had come home by that time and was taken prisoner and forced to ride south with General McBride's units. McBride hoped to meet up with General McCullough and then to march on Springfield, where Lyon and Sigel were camped. Near the Arkansas border, Monks managed to escape his captors. Monks made his way toward Springfield to join Federal forces, sleeping in ditches and avoiding Confederate scouts. On his way back through Howell County, he was stopped by a lady outside a house a few hours before daylight. She invited him in, and as he approached the door, he was met by a man with an old Springfield musket and wearing his nightgown, inquiring as to the balance of Monks's party and his intentions. He assured the man he was alone and had been held captive by the Confederates and was trying to get to Springfield to the Union camp. Surveying Monks's condition, he set the rifle down and invited him inside. Monks was informed that there were refugee wagons a couple of miles away, ready to head to Springfield, and the couple would get him there in time to leave with the wagons. The wife offered him a bed to rest but Monks declined, saying he wasn't fit to rest in a bed, having slept on the ground since his capture. The reply was that she didn't care how dirty a Union man was, he was welcome to the bed.

After eating breakfast, Monks's host said his captain lived just this side of where the wagons were camped and would love to see Monks and hear about the movements of the Rebels. The man took him to his captain's house, where the captain asked his name, where he was from and the circumstances of his capture. Upon hearing that Monks was from Howell County, the man asked him if he was acquainted with a Washington Galloway and on which side was Galloway. Monks replied that he did know Galloway and that he was a captain commanding one of the Rebel companies under McBride. Monks had had a conversation with Galloway the night before Monks had escaped. The captain said that Galloway was his brother and then introduced himself as Jesse Galloway, tears running from his eyes. He allowed Monks to rest and then had one of his men take him to Springfield by horseback. About three weeks after Monks left Jesse Galloway's house, Rebels surrounded Galloway's home and hid until he walked out into the yard, where they shot him while he was holding a child.

After Monks was taken prisoner by General McBride's men, his wife sold what property she could at "Confederate prices" and took their five small children to Rolla. Mrs. Monks enlisted the help of Colonel John S. Phelps, of Springfield, to locate her husband. Phelps, not having information of Monks, placed an advertisement in newspapers of the arrival of Mrs. Monks in Rolla in an attempt to get word to Monks of his family's whereabouts. The news did reach Monks, who was at that point in Randolph County, Illinois. He set out for Rolla to find his wife and children, living in one of the army tents vacated by the army moving west to Springfield. Monks spent the rest of the war recruiting men for the Union army and was made captain of Company K of the Sixteenth Missouri Cavalry.

Hospitality and cooperation were not insurance against violence either. In early 1862, about fifteen men with a Rebel scout came to the home of Sampson Mawhinney, a Union man. Mawhinney and his wife fed the men dinner, and Mawhinney even shod their horses. Afterward, the men told Mawhinney they were arresting him. His wife protested that surely they would not hurt him after feeding them and caring for the horses. She received no reply. A mile down the road, the scout took Mawhinney off the road and shot him. His wife retrieved his body and buried him.

Home Guard militia units were formed in many towns and were operated independently of the regular armies but were aligned with one side or the other. Reenactment photo. *Courtesy of Alex Martin.*

As a result of the violence, Howell County became depopulated, like many other counties in the region. What was left were roaming bands of bushwhackers pillaging homes and businesses for whatever they could find of value to them. West Plains was burned by the Rebels to keep the Federals from using it as a military post. There was violence on both sides, but the Union never had a strong presence in Howell County, and Union men in the area had no choice but to leave their homes with only what they could carry. Many people died of exposure in the winter of 1861 trying to reach shelter and safety at Rolla, Missouri. It was said that in that part of southern Missouri, no Union families remained between Rolla in central Missouri and Batesville, Arkansas, at the border. Those families on either side who did remain were left without men, the women often sheltering their children in the woods for safety, hunting with rifles and foraging berries to stave off starvation.

The experience of Benjamin Alsup, who had been a county judge and representative in the state legislature, provides a vivid example of consequences of not taking the oath of allegiance. Alsup was a civilian and had not taken up arms, but he was a strong Union man. In 1862, he was

Ghostly Civil War soldiers are reported in many places in southwest Missouri. This is a photo created by using specific lighting and exposure techniques to transform reenactors into ghostly visions. *Courtesy of Alex Martin.*

taken prisoner and held in Little Rock, Arkansas. The Confederate guerrilla leader from Jasper County, Thomas Livingston, unsuccessfully attempted to negotiate Alsup's exchange for Confederates held prisoner in a letter written to a Union commander on June 15, 1862. Instead, Alsup was held for three years. He was forced to work in a bark mill next to a blind mule, a strap around his chest and leather handholds on each hand, pulling along with the mule. As a result of the forced labor, he lost most use of one hand for the rest of his life. At the end of the war, he was traded for some Southern prisoners.

THE BATTLE OF
WILSON'S CREEK

After the Battle of Carthage, Sigel retreated and established headquarters in Mount Vernon, where he awaited Lyon to reach the southwest. The two forces joined up at Springfield and awaited the impending fight. General Sterling Price's Missouri State Guard forces camped at Neosho. Lyon knew that his men were outnumbered, especially with the Arkansas regular Confederate forces under General McCullough reinforcing Price's Missourians. Lyon requested reinforcements from General Fremont, who declined to approve the request, leaving Lyon and Sigel to face an enemy that greatly outnumbered the Federals.

Lyon was faced with two choices: retreat from southwest Missouri and allow Price to take it without a fight, or take the fight to Price directly, relying upon his superior artillery and discipline of his better-trained army to tip the scales in his favor. Retreat probably did not enter Lyon's mind as an option, based upon his actions up to that point. Favoring a fight on open ground, Lyon marched his men ten miles south of Springfield to Crane Creek on a hot late afternoon, August 1, 1861. The march resumed in the morning, with skirmishes en route to Dug Springs. Shells from the Federal battery scattered the Rebel advances. Confederate infantry attempted to cut off the Federal cavalry by approaching through the woods but were spotted. Union cavalry opened fire with Sharpe's carbines. The Rebel infantry outnumbered the Federal cavalry of one hundred by five to one. A Union lieutenant gave orders for a unit of twenty-five men to charge into the Rebel line of bayonets. The small unit was successful in breaking the line, which had outnumbered them, twenty to one. When additional Federals reached the line, they found wounded Rebels asking whether "these were men or devils, they fight so." Artillery then sent the remaining Rebels from the field, resulting in a Federal victory with only five casualties and four wounded, while the Confederates incurred forty killed and more than one hundred wounded.

Lyon continued on to Curran (pronounced *kurn*), in Stone County, about twenty-six miles southwest of Springfield. Facing a potential flanking maneuver to cut his communication with Springfield, his men exhausted in the brutal heat and a thin supply line—which had to come from Rolla, more than one hundred miles to the north—Lyon was not in a position to push the Rebels farther south. He returned to Springfield to await the enemy. Again, Lyon had to ponder whether to retreat to Rolla as requests for reinforcements continued to be ignored, while knowing that Price and McCullough had vastly superior numbers of men and, in particular, cavalry, which meant that a retreat was likely to entail either defending the immense supply and refugee train he would have with him or taking a stand in the southwest.

The night of August 9, 1861, General Nathaniel Lyon sent Major Franz Sigel and about five thousand men to surround the Missouri State Guard forces of General Sterling Price and regular Confederate forces from Arkansas under General McCullough, which numbered about twelve thousand, which were camped along Wilson's Creek ten miles southwest of Springfield. At daylight, the larger Confederate force overtook Sigel's men, and Lyon's reinforcements, arriving in the morning hours, were unable to contain the larger force. Lyon is noted for valiant fighting that day, wounded twice before his horse was shot out from under him. Undeterred, Lyon personally led another charge on the Confederate line and was shot and killed. Lyon's army retreated some one hundred miles to the northeast to Rolla, and southwest Missouri was left in the hands of Price's army until Federal forces retook Springfield the following February after victory at the Battle of Pea Ridge, Arkansas. The spot where it is believed that General Lyon fell from his horse was soon marked by a large pile of stones. This became a historic site well before the battlefield became a national park.

Franz Sigel described the circumstances of his retreat after the war:

> *So we marched, or rather dragged along as fast as the exhausted men could go, until we reached the ford at James Fork of the White River. Carr had*

already crossed, but his cavalry was not in sight; it had hastened along without waiting for us; a part of the infantry had also passed the creek; the piece and caissons were just crossing, when the rattling of musketry announced the presence of hostile forces on both sides of the creek. They were detachments of Missouri and Texas cavalry, under Lieutenant-Colonel Major, Captains Mabry and Russell, that lay in ambush, and now pounced upon our jaded and extended column. It was in vain that Lieutenant-Colonel Albert and myself tried to rally at least a part of them; they left the road to seek protection, or make good their escape in the woods, and were followed and hunted down by their pursuers. In this chase the greater part of our men were killed, wounded, or made prisoners, among the latter Lieutenant-Colonel Albert and my orderly, who were with me in the last moment of the affray. I was not taken, probably because I wore a blue woolen blanket over my uniform and a yellowish slouch-hat, giving me the appearance of a Texas Ranger. I halted on horseback, prepared for defense, in a small strip of corn-field on the west side of the creek, while the hostile cavalrymen swarmed around and several times passed close by me. When we had resumed our way toward the north-east, we were immediately recognized as enemies, and pursued by a few horsemen, whose number increased rapidly. It was a pretty lively race for about six miles, when our pursuers gave up the chase. We reached Springfield at 4:30 in the afternoon, in advance of Sturgis, who with Lyon's troops was retreating from the battle-field, and who arrived at Springfield, as he says, at 5 o'clock. The circumstance of my arrival at the time stated gave rise to the insinuation that I had forsaken my troops after their repulse at Sharp's house, and had delivered them to their fate. Spiced with the accusation of "plunder," this and other falsehoods were repeated before the Committee on the Conduct of the War, and a letter defamatory of me was dispatched to the Secretary of War (dated February 14th, 1862, six months after the battle of Wilson's Creek). I had no knowledge of these calumnies against me until long after the war, when I found them in print. In support of my statements, I would direct attention to my own reports on the battle and to the Confederate reports, especially to those of Lieutenant-Colonel Hyams and Captain Vigilini, of the 3d Louisiana; also to the report of Captain Carr, in which he frankly states that he abandoned me immediately before my column was attacked at the crossing of James Fork, without notifying me of the approach of the enemy's cavalry.

The Battle of Wilson's Creek

The Battle of Wilson's Creek involved close hand-to-hand combat in the midst of tranquil farmland. Reenactment photo. *Courtesy of L. Edward Martin.*

Confederate Brigadier General N.B. Pearce also recounted Wilson's Creek, or as he referred to it, the Battle of Oak Hills, as was the common Confederate name for the battle:

> *In the early morning…General Sigel, commanding the left column of the advance from Springfield, came upon our right and rear, first attacking Colonel Churchill's camp, as the men were preparing for breakfast, obliging them to retreat to an adjacent wood, where they were formed in good order. The surprise resulted from the movement of the night before, when pickets had been withdrawn that were not re-posted in the morning. Sigel did not wait for a fight, however, but advanced to, and had his battery unlimbered near, the Fayetteville road, west of Wilson's Creek, opposite and within range of Reid's battery as it was then in position as originally placed. Before he had discovered us, and perhaps in ignorance of our position, Reid attacked him, under my personal orders and supervision. Sigel's movement was a bold one, and we really could not tell, on his first appearance (there*

having been no fight with Churchill), whether he was friend or foe. An accidental gust of wind having unfurled his flag, we were no longer in doubt. Reid succeeded in getting his range accurately, so that his shot proved very effective. At this juncture, General McCulloch in person led two companies of the Louisiana infantry in a charge and captured five of the guns. General Sigel was himself in command, and made vain attempts to hold his men, who were soon in full retreat, back over the road they came, pursued by the Texas and Missouri cavalry. This was the last of Sigel for the day, as his retreat was continued to Springfield. As a precaution, however, not knowing how badly we had defeated Sigel, I immediately posted the 4th Arkansas Infantry (Colonel Walker) along the brow of the hill, commanding the road over which he had fled, which regiment remained on duty until the battle was over…

The fight "mit Sigel" had resulted satisfactorily to us, but the troops more immediately opposed to General Lyon had not done so well. General Price and his Missouri troops had borne the brunt of this hard contest, but had gained no ground. They had suffered heavy losses, and were running short of ammunition. I had watched anxiously for signs of victory to come from the north side of the creek, but Totten's battery seemed to belch forth with renewed vigor, and was advanced once or twice in its position. The line of battle on our left was shortening, and the fortunes of war appeared to be sending many of our gallant officers and soldiers to their death. There was no demoralization—no signs of wavering or retreat, but it was an hour of great anxiety and suspense. No one then knew what the day would bring forth. As the sun poured down upon our devoted comrades, poised and resting, as it were, between the chapters of a mighty struggle not yet completed, the stoutest of us almost weakened in our anxiety to know the outcome. Just at this time, General Lyon appeared to be massing his men for a final and decisive movement. I had been relieved of Sigel, and Reid's battery was inactive because it could not reach Totten. This was fortunate, for my command, in a measure fresh and enthusiastic, was about to embrace an opportunity—such a one as will often win or lose a battle—by throwing its strength to the weakened line at a critical moment and winning the day. Colonel McIntosh came to me from General McCulloch, and Captain Greene from General Price, urging me to move at once to their assistance. General Lyon was in possession of Oak Hill; his lines were forward, his batteries aggressive, and his charges impetuous.

The Battle of Wilson's Creek

The fortunes of the day were balanced in the scale, and something must be done or the battle was lost…a combined advance was ordered by General McCulloch. This proved to be the decisive engagement, and as volley after volley was poured against our lines, and our gallant boys were cut down like grass, those who survived seemed to be nerved to greater effort and a determination to win or die. At about this time (11:30 A.M.) the first line of battle before us gave way. Our boys charged the second line with a yell, and were soon in possession of the field, the enemy slowly withdrawing toward Springfield. This hour decided the contest and won for us the day. It was in our front here, as was afterward made known, that the brave commander of the Federal forces, General Lyon, was killed, gallantly leading his men to what he and they supposed was victory, but which proved (it may be because they were deprived of his enthusiastic leadership) disastrous defeat. In the light of the present day, even, it is difficult to measure the vast results had Lyon lived and the battle gone against us… We watched the retreating enemy through our field-glasses, and were glad to see him go. Our ammunition was exhausted, our men undisciplined, and we feared to risk pursuit.

As the day wore on, artillery noise and smoke created confusion during the battle. Reenactment photo. *Courtesy of L. Edward Martin.*

47

The summit of the ridge where Lyon and many others on each side fell is now known as Bloody Hill. While Lyon became the first general to die in combat during the Civil War, it is the phantom specters of Confederate soldiers and cavalry that are most often seen by visitors on Bloody Hill, which is now part of the Wilson's Creek Battlefield National Park. Mounted cavalry are seen silently charging across Bloody Hill in scenes similarly experienced at other Civil War battlefields such as Gettysburg, where visitors are confronted with drilling units and make the mistaken assumption that they are watching Civil War reenactors performing for visitors, only to later find that there were no such activities going on that day. However, local residents and visitors to the battlefield have also witnessed groups of soldiers in Union uniforms walking near Bloody Hill and other spots along Wilson's Creek, only to vanish into thin air. Another apparition reported by visitors is that of a young woman walking up the grassy hill from the springhouse toward the Ray House in a long period dress with a water bucket in her hand. Visitors have called to the woman, assuming she was an actor in a living museum program, but she does not respond, continuing on her path through prairie grass. Upon inquiring of park personnel, the witnesses learn there that were no programs that day and no woman acting out a role.

The farmhouse belonging to John Ray was in the line of fire as the fighting at Wilson's Creek was about to commence. According to the National Park Service's description of events, early on the morning of August 10, 1861, the Ray family's world turned upside down. Three of the Ray children, herding horses in the valley near the springhouse, were warned by a soldier on horseback that "there's going to be fighting like hell in less than ten minutes." After being informed of the soldier's warning, Roxanna Ray took her children, slaves—including Aunt Rhoda and her children—and hired hand Julius Short into the cellar. Meanwhile, John Ray watched the fighting between U.S. Regulars and Arkansas and Louisiana troops in their cornfield. Soon the Confederates forced the Union from the field, but Union artillery fire from Bloody Hill drove the Confederates back past the Ray House. The Union battery continued to fire and, in the process, hit the Ray chicken house. Southern surgeons raised a yellow flag (recognized on the battlefield as a symbol of a field hospital), and the gunners ceased fire. The Ray House itself was not struck during the battle.

When the battle ended, the family found their farmhouse was now a hospital and immediately began to assist medical personnel in treating the wounded and dying. The children made many trips to secure water from the springhouse for the suffering soldiers. Later, the body of General Nathaniel Lyon was brought to the house and examined before it was removed under a flag of truce. Roxanna supplied a counterpane, or bedspread, to cover the body. While most of the wounded were quickly removed to Springfield, one soldier would convalesce with the Rays for several weeks before he could be moved. In addition, most of the family's livestock and crops were gone, foraged by hungry soldiers.

General Nathaniel Lyon at the Battle of Wilson's Creek, as appeared in *Harper's Weekly*. The caption refers to Lyon at the Battle of Springfield, demonstrating that there was not always consistency in the references to Civil War battles. *Courtesy of Victorian Carthage, LLC, Kendrick House collection.*

General Lyon's body was taken to Springfield, to the home of U.S. congressman and colonel in the Missouri Home Guard, Union forces, John S. Phelps, where Mrs. Phelps buried his body in her root cellar to avoid detection by the Confederate army, which now had control of the city. Later, after the Federal army retook control of the town, Lyon's body was exhumed and taken to his native Connecticut on a funeral train, with stops in cities such as Cincinnati, New York, Philadelphia and Hartford.

The number of surgeries and amputations performed at the Ray house was so large that the amputated limbs were discarded in looming piles outside the Ray farmhouse. The Rebel army retired to Springfield and took up the fortifications vacated by the Federal retreat. John Ray was left with the unpleasant task of burying the discarded amputated limbs that lay outside the house in the sweltering heat of August in southwest Missouri, where it can easily rise to one hundred degrees for days on end. Ray, weary from this task thrust upon his family, sent a letter to the Confederate command in Springfield some weeks later asking if a detail could not be sent to assist in the job of burying the remains, as he and his family had been unable to keep ahead of the decomposing limbs. Today, the John Ray House is part of Wilson's Creek National Battlefield Park; it and the Rays' springhouse are the only surviving structures on the battlefield. The Ray House was used as a private residence until the 1960s, when it was sold to the National Park Service.

The Ray House was built on the Wire or Telegraph Road that ran from Jefferson City, Missouri, to Fort Smith, Arkansas, passing through Springfield, Missouri. It was so called due to the fact that telegraph wire was strung along the road in 1860. In the 1850s, the Butterfield Overland Stage Company used the road as part of its route from Missouri to California, and the Ray House served as a flag stop for the stagecoaches. During the war, the road became a military road for Federal and Confederate troops for operations in the Ozark region. In February 1862, Confederate troops marched the Wire Road on their way to the Battle of Pea Ridge, where they were defeated and official Confederate control of southern Missouri was lost, although Confederate guerrilla units continued to effectively operate throughout the war.

The Rays also illustrated that in Missouri, owning slaves did not necessarily make one a secessionist or Confederate sympathizer. The Rays were unconditional Unionists, and in fact, John Ray held the Federal contract as postmaster throughout the war, which would not have occurred if there was suspicion of his loyalty to the Federal government. Another striking example of this seemingly paradoxical position is Congressman John S. Phelps and his wife, Mary, of nearby Springfield. John S. Phelps was a lawyer, a member of Missouri's House of Representatives (elected in 1840) and the United States House of Representatives (elected in 1844) and a Union soldier. With the outbreak of the Civil War, John Phelps became colonel of the Greene County Regiment, Missouri Home Guard. Following the Union defeat at Wilson's Creek, Phelps was appointed colonel of Phelps's Regiment, Missouri Infantry, and a six-month unit that fought at the Battle of Pea Ridge. Even though a prominent Unionist, Congressman Phelps owned slaves.

SPRINGFIELD, MISSOURI

CIVIL WAR HEADQUARTERS

At the outset of the Civil War, Springfield was more Southern in its sympathies but served as Union headquarters from the time of the Battle of Carthage until the Confederate victory at the Battle of Wilson's Creek on August 10, 1861. Wilson's Creek involved more than 17,000 troops. Federal casualties were about 1,139, and Confederate casualties were about 1,245. Compare these numbers to those at the First Battle of Bull Run, which was the largest and bloodiest battle in American history up to that point, with Federal casualties of 2,950 and Confederate casualties of 1,750, but involved more than three times as many men, with more than 60,000 combatants.

As the Federal army retreated to Rolla, a move which General Lyon tried so stringently to avoid, many civilian Union sympathizers abandoned their homes, and the roads were clogged with wagons headed north toward Rolla behind Rebel lines. Secessionists throughout Missouri were emboldened by the defeat of the Union army at Wilson's Creek and the death of Lyon, resulting in an escalation of attacks upon Federal troops and supply trains, as well as upon Union sympathizers, even resulting in martial law being declared in the Federal stronghold of St. Louis. As for the southwest portion of the state, the Confederates were in full control, with the violence only beginning.

Downtown Springfield is filled with Civil War sites. The old courthouse on the square was used as a military hospital for four years and wounded from the Battles of Carthage and Wilson's Creek were treated there. The square would also be the scene of one of the most iconic gunfights in America, arising out of tensions of two soldiers, one Union and one Confederate, with a dispute over a card game bringing it to confrontation.

Charles Butler Hickok, better known as Wild Bill Hickok, was a Union scout and spy who, prior to the outbreak of the war, had served the army in bloody Kansas, defending the slaveholding settlers there from the violence of the abolitionists, exemplified by Jim Lane's Redlegs and John Brown's retaliatory massacres in eastern Kansas and extreme western Missouri. Characteristic of many men who fought in this region, friendships often transcended politics. After the end of hostilities in the spring of 1865, Hickok remained in Springfield, Missouri, spending much of his time at poker tables. He became friends with Dave Tutt, a former Confederate soldier, but that friendship turned deadly in July 1865 when an argument erupted between the two over allegations of cheating at cards. The argument led to one of the most infamous gunfights in American history and one of the few that resembled the iconic images of Hollywood—two gunfighters facing off one on one in the open. The two met on the square, which in many respects appears much the same as it did then: an open interior square with streets framing the square and buildings lining the outer sides of the streets. On the northwest corner stood the Greene County Courthouse, which had seen direct service in the Civil War as the general hospital for the Union army. Tutt stood in front of the courthouse, and Hickok stood on the southeast corner of the square. Hickok shot Tutt, who turned and staggered to the courthouse steps, falling and exclaiming, "I'm dead, boys," before dying. The events were covered in *Harper's Weekly* and propelled Hickok to fame. The shootout also led to Hickok being tried for murder, which is reenacted for the public periodically and provides a glimpse into early justice in the American West. More than twenty witnesses who were present on the square at the time of the gunfight were called to testify, but only four admitted to actually seeing any of the fight firsthand. Even of those four, some claimed they did not see Hickok pull the trigger of his rifle. It was unclear whether Tutt had gotten off a shot before he was hit. One witness said that although he could not see either man shoot from his position, he heard only one shot. Perhaps out of frontier practicality or an unknown motive, Hickok was acquitted of all charges, despite the fact that he had walked onto the square with a loaded rifle with the announced intent of engaging in a gunfight with Tutt.

While the old courthouse is long gone and now the empty, old Heers Department Store building stands in its place, the events and intense emotions of the Civil War, and those who fought in it on this place, may have had a lasting impression. There have long been stories of ghosts on the square, even after the area lost its prominence and luster, with only a portion of the buildings used. In the 1980s, it was home to Springfield's homeless, and apparitions were observed roaming the neglected square, perhaps soldiers still on picket or returning from a scouting party, although long dead; perhaps Dave Tutt, eternally replaying his final moments; or perhaps soldiers treated as patients for wounds incurred at the Battles of Carthage or Wilson's Creek. I recall stories of hauntings of the Heers Department Store building from that time period, including the presence of apparitions, unexplained noises and the feeling of being watched or a general unease.

The Stephens Academy, the first academy in Greene County, was established by Professor J.A. Stephens in 1845 and was located near the current TraveLodge Motel at 505 St. Louis Street. Stephens Academy existed until Christmas Day 1861, when its principal met a tragic death. The city was being threatened, and zealous, tense soldiers cried, "Halt!" at John Andrew Stephens as he walked from downtown to his home in the 300 block of Mount Vernon Street. He had been warned of danger in doing so but said that he must go to his wife and daughters. Hard of hearing, he did not hear the command, and he was shot and killed by the soldiers.

There are stories of ghosts on Stephens's land, including accounts of mysterious sightings in the area, which during the mid-1800s was a cemetery. The cemetery was moved to allow for development of the land as the city grew, but on at least two occasions, graves and human remains have been unearthed. By the 1880s, the old cemetery was in decline and overgrown. Lewdon Sawyer, a grandson of Mr. Stephens, told stories of how as a boy he and the neighbor children would take one of the markers out of the cemetery and erect it over the grave of any pet, whether it be chicken or dog, that might die in the neighborhood. Many small boys were afraid to go by the place after nightfall, for there were tales of ghosts that roamed there and queer lights.

There were fortifications and skirmishes fought throughout modern-day Springfield, including the grounds of Drury College, which was established in 1873 as Springfield College and shortly after renamed Drury College. It was built on the site of Civil War fortifications, including a low ridge behind

University Plaza, Springfield, Missouri, part of present-day Springfield built on top of the site of Civil War fortifications and skirmishes. The ghost of the "Colonel," thought to be Colonel John S. Phelps, is observed walking the halls and lobby. *Courtesy of Alex Martin.*

Burnham Hall, the administration building, which is actually the effaced remains of the Union rifle pits. The fortifications in turn were built atop old Indian burial mounds near the soccer fields. Cannons used in Civil War operations here also line the approach to Burnham Hall. Confederate dead from the Battle of Wilson's Creek, estimated to be as many as five hundred, were buried in unmarked graves on and near the present-day campus. Drury has various legends of paranormal activity in several buildings, including poltergeist activity of objects being moved and music heard playing.

A Civil War ghost is seen roaming the University Plaza hotel just a few blocks from Drury University. He is seen wandering the hallways and sitting in the spacious lobby. He wears an officer's uniform and is referred to as the "Colonel." The common belief is that this is the ghost of Union Colonel John S. Phelps. It is not farfetched to think he would wander the area. Much of downtown Springfield, including the site of University Plaza and the square, was once part of his large farm of 1,200 acres. The Colonel is not a frightening ghost, and employees refer to him in fond tones. He appears to be watching over his land even now.

GUERRILLA WARFARE
SOUTHWEST MISSOURI BECOMES THE "BURNT DISTRICT"

Nevada, Missouri, was known as the bushwhacker capital, as there was such widespread and intense guerrilla activity in Vernon County. The area had already lost a lot of population due to raids from Kansas abolitionists prior to the war. The situation only worsened with official combat. While women—including teenager Myra Shirley, later known as Belle Starr—throughout southwest Missouri engaged in spying and carrying information to units in the field, particularly guerrilla units, women were more hands-on in the war in Vernon County. There were several renowned female bushwhackers who actively participated in guerrilla warfare, including the Mayfield family. The Union army employed a scorched earth policy in Vernon County fairly early on in the war in retaliation for the bushwhackers' operations in adjoining counties in Kansas, including the two burnings of the town of Humboldt, Kansas. The bushwhackers' attacks in Kansas were, in turn, a response to the raids by Kansans in Missouri. With many murders and lynchings, it is not surprising that there are Civil War ghosts in the area.

Present-day Cottey College, a women's college, in Nevada, Missouri, did not exist during the Civil War. While it sits in the middle of town now, the college's land was farmland and was located almost a mile from town in the 1860s. Much of the land was owned by a Confederate soldier. It is believed that Cottey's Blanche Skiff Ross Memorial Library sits on the site of the old farmhouse. Cottey College has become the site of several interrelated ghost

Cottey College's Blanche Skiff Ross Memorial Library, only the latest building on this spot, sits on the site of a Civil War–era farmhouse. Later the Amerman Sanatorium was on this site before being purchased by Cottey College. *Courtesy of L. Edward Martin.*

stories that seem to share an apparition from the Civil War days, although at least some of the other apparitions are from later periods.

One of the most infamous apparitions is the Black Spirit, which is an elderly black man who is believed to be the ghost of a slave who lived in the area. He is often seen in Reeves Hall, one of the residence halls, as well as other locations, and seems attracted to women with dark hair and glasses who tend to be music majors. He is seen sitting on the ends of their beds or in a desk chair if it is left pulled out, and some say he can be violent. Some believe that he is looking for a specific student, Vera Alice Neitzert, a music student who died tragically on May 17, 1920, of severe burns received when her nightgown caught fire while she and friends were making candy in a chafing dish in a suite sitting room in Main Hall. She was taken to the Amerman Sanatorium, a hospital that stood where the Blanche Skiff Ross Memorial Library was later built. Vera died at the hospital a few days later and is said to roam Main Hall and Rosemary Hall—where music would be heard playing until it was torn down—and all over the campus. The fact that the Black Spirit focuses on music students has led to the speculation that he is looking for the unfortunate Vera. While some may say that is illogical because they lived in different time periods and appear in buildings that did not exist during their presumed lifetimes, it is my experience that ghosts are not fixed to a particular building, and activity from different time periods is not that unusual.

Ross Library also is the site of unexplained music, as well as poltergeist activity such as books falling off shelves and book carts rolling on their own. An old man is seen in a smoking jacket on the balcony. Other activity in the library includes two girls in 1800s dress who play on the stairs. Housekeepers have observed a young woman in a long white gown reading a book in the early hours before the building opens and have had their linen closets rearranged inexplicably. Whether these ghosts are from the Civil War period, when the area was a working farm, or a later time period is not known for sure.

Some believe that the piano music heard in different buildings is being played by Madame Blitz, head of Cottey's music department in the early 1900s. In 1904, Madame Blitz drank carbolic acid and died in her home across the street from Cottey's Main Hall, and her spirit is said to walk the campus. Madame Blitz would utilize practice rooms for students in buildings across the campus, so it may make sense that she still plays music in various locations.

Another tragic incident at Cottey College may account for some of the activity. For the fall semester of 1915, Grace Innis, a local girl who had suffered severe illness for half her life, was admitted to Cottey. She seemed to be happy and adjusting well until December 20, 1915, when she went to her mother's house in Nevada for the holidays. While her mother went shopping, Grace called Howard & Cress Garage for a car to drive her to Miller & Hopkins Drug Store, where she purchased bottles of carbolic acid, ether and milk of magnesia. Miss Grace directed the driver to drop her off at Cottey, and she then walked to Radio Spring Park eight blocks away.

Miss Uhler, walking home from school, saw Grace going down the East Hill toward the lake. A few minutes later, Miss Uhler and her mother heard screams coming from the park. They ran out of their home to find Grace, wet, wringing her hands and crying that she had taken carbolic acid. It was assumed that Grace drank the acid and then waded into the lake, where the cold water shocked her back to her senses. The Uhlers helped Grace to their home and called for a doctor. When Drs. Yater and Williams arrived, they realized that little could be done for the girl. Although "everything was done not only to save her life but to relieve her sufferings which were terrible," Grace Innis passed away in the cottage at 7:30 p.m. Grace's hat and muff were later found on the ground by the springboard. While it is not known why she took her life, it is presumed that the stress of her long illness likely played a part.

THOMAS R. LIVINGSTON, SOUTHWEST MISSOURI GUERRILLA LEADER

T homas R. Livingston, as discussed previously, was a secessionist from the outset. His experiences in southwest Missouri's warfare are a good illustration of the complex relation between the guerrilla fighters, regular troops and the civilian population. Livingston had broad mining interests in southwest Missouri. He owned the mine at Minersville (now Oronogo) in western Jasper County, which in time became the largest pit, lead and zinc mine in the world, now known as Oronogo Circle. When the war broke out, it is said that Livingston dumped several thousand pounds of molten lead into Center Creek at his smelter in Minersville to prevent approaching Federal troops from confiscating it for making ammunition. He and his half brother, William Parkinson, also had a lead smelter at French Point, several miles west of Minersville, as well as a store and mill.

Livingston also held stakes in the lead mines at Granby, in Newton County, to the south, which at the outbreak of the war was the largest producing lead-mining district in southwest Missouri. The Confederate army occupied Granby until it was forced out of southwest Missouri after the Battle of Pea Ridge, Arkansas, in 1862. The strategic value of the Granby mines was such that official Confederate reports tracked the tonnage of lead being shipped to Fort Smith, Arkansas, and points east. The commanding officer in Granby was confident that the Granby mines would supply the Confederacy's demand for lead for bullets. Each month, 200,000 pounds of lead were shipped from Granby. Livingston owned one of the four smelters in Granby and, by some accounts, at least one of the saloons as well. He also had business ties in Indian Territory, present-day Oklahoma. As discussed, Livingston had a reputation of being good-natured but willing and able to effectively fight. It was reported by the *Bolivar Weekly Courier* on April 14, 1860, that an attempt on the life of Captain Tom Livingston was made by John Tutt, a "desperate type," at Granby.

As said previously, Livingston was drilling a militia unit before the war was officially declared and had been a captain in the Missouri militia for several years. He was well respected and well liked by the men who fought under him. George B. Walker, a local resident, gave his recollection of Thomas Livingston after the war. He said Livingston "never knew fear and his men during the war idolized him. They said that there was never a leader so good to his men as Major Tom Livingston." His enlistment having expired in the Missouri State Guard, Livingston returned home and enlisted his men in the Provisional Army of the Confederate States, designated as the First Battalion Missouri Cavalry (First Indian Brigade). The group would come to be known as the Cherokee Spikes or Bloody Spikes.

By late July 1861, Livingston and his men were patrolling the Missouri-Kansas border and also protecting the lead mines at Granby and Minersville. By September, Livingston was cooperating with the Confederate partisan ranger John Matthews, who lived in Labette County, Kansas, and raided Humboldt, Kansas, which is southwest of Fort Scott, the principal Federal military installation along the Missouri-Kansas border. The town had been used as a base for Federal scouts along the border who had raided and burned Missouri towns. The town was burned, and horses and other property were seized. Not long afterward, Lieutenant Colonel James Blunt pursued John Matthews to the Quapaw Indian Agency, in Indian Territory, killed Matthews and scattered his men. Livingston was sent back to Humboldt as revenge for Matthews's death. Confederate general McCullough made raiding into Kansas a part of his overall strategy, but the residents were allowed to remove property from their homes before the town was torched, and it was ordered that no men in the town be executed. McCullough also sent the Cherokee general (then still a colonel) Stand Waitie, based in Indian Territory, to move into Kansas and "destroy everything." Although he reported directly to Waite, Livingston did not return to Kansas again but focused on border patrol, guarding and working the Granby mines, escorting lead shipments to Fort Smith, reconnaissance securing information on Federal troop and supply train movements. It also appears from correspondence of General Price that Livingston recruited men among the Osage Indians.

While Livingston had been a secessionist even before the war's start, it did not mean his allegiance was blind. As the war wore on and the Confederacy failed to devote resources to the border area, onlookers were surprised to hear Livingston speak publicly in Mount Vernon, Missouri, between Carthage and Springfield, where he stated that in his opinion, the Confederate army had not kept its assurances to help protect southwest Missouri and lamented that the secessionist cause had left southwest Missouri in a vulnerable position, without adequate support to protect the civilians in the area. Likewise, Livingston sent requests to the Confederate command requesting additional resources and men to prevent the people from being put in further peril. His frustration grew, as can be seen in his correspondence, and as time went on, he began sending requests directly to General Price, bypassing his direct superiors. Livingston engaged in negotiations with Union commanders operating in the region, attempting to secure mutual assurances to not disrupt farmers and to allow planting of crops without the risk of fields being torched. These actions indicate that Livingston had motives beyond mere plunder, revenge or military objectives. They also drew the condemnation of some of the Confederate officers.

The event that stands out the most in Thomas R. Livingston's operations is the Rader Farm massacre in western Jasper County, Missouri, and the consequences of the events there. Fort Blair, a wooden fort, had been built in Baxter Springs, Kansas, by the Union army as a means of protecting the supply trains traveling the military road between Fort Scott, Kansas, some fifty miles north, and Fort Gibson, Indian Territory, approximately one hundred miles to the south. Fort Blair sat a mere fifteen miles inside Kansas and due west of central Jasper County, including Livingston's concerns at Minersville.

The Union raised an all-black regiment at Baxter Springs, the First Kansas Colored Infantry, many of whom were escaped slaves from southwest Missouri. These black troops were under the command of James Williams. The First Kansas was the second colored unit officially mustered into service for the Union but was the first colored unit to see combat and suffer casualties in the Civil War, in October 1862, at the Battle of Mound Island, near Butler, Bates County, Missouri, along the northern edge of the burnt district in southwest Missouri.

Lisa Livingston-Martin at the site of Fort Blair, Baxter Springs, Kansas, where the black soldiers killed at the Rader Farm were stationed. Fort Blair was a timber fort and was destroyed at the Battle of Baxter Springs in 1864. *Courtesy of L. Edward Martin.*

Williams was anxious to prove the ability of his men, and perhaps this contributed to a rash decision to send them into Jasper County on May 6, 1863, to forage for food. The column was hard to miss, with wagons, infantry and cavalry—a column that seems ill-suited for foraging for food behind enemy lines. The troops raided homes, taking a carding machine that was used to turn cotton into thread, and Mrs. Scott, the lady of the house, was held for a time. A wagon of flour on its way to Livingston's men was taken from a young boy driving the wagon, who also was held and later released along with Mrs. Scott. After capturing twenty horses and mules, two local women rode into the Federal line. When asked by Major Ward, the commanding officer of the foraging party, what they were doing, they responded that they were counting his men to tell Livingston how many soldiers were camped. Ward confiscated the ladies' horses, and while walking out of the Federal camp, the ladies left with the parting words that they were still delivering the information to Livingston. The next morning, the women returned and demanded the return of their horses and saddles. Ward again refused their demand, and they complained loudly and in particular to Hugh

Troops often found themselves foraging for food and supplies while operating in southwest Missouri, leading to much hardship of the people living in the region and contributing to animosities. Reenactment photo. *Courtesy of L. Edward Martin.*

Thompson, one of the Union soldiers whom they knew, threatening that Livingston and his men would hang him upon their return. Next, Williams's men camped at the home of R.R. Twitty, one of Livingston's men, and took three hundred pounds of bacon, a calf and corn from Twitty's mother.

Williams didn't merely send the men into Missouri—he sent them to Sherwood, which was the third-largest town in Jasper County and known as a strong Confederate enclave. Many of the men fighting under Livingston lived in Sherwood. Williams didn't stop there; on May 11, 1863, he sent an insulting letter to Livingston, in which he failed to even address Livingston by name:

To Commanding officer of Southern forces in Jasper & Newton County, MO,

Sir,

I came here by order of my Superiors under instructions to put a stop to the Guerilla or Bushwacking war which is now being carried out by the enemies of the United States in Jasper and Newton Counties, MO. It is my desire in this Business to follow as far as practicable all the rules applicable to Civilized warfare. I therefore propose that you collect all the enemies of the United States in your vicinity and come to some point and attack me, or give me notice where I can find your force and I will fight you on your own ground.

But if you persist in the System of Guerilla warfare heretofore followed by you and refuse to fight openly like soldiers fighting for a cause I feel bound to treat you as thieves and robbers who lurk in secret places fighting only defenseless people and wholly unworthy the fate due to Chivalrous Soldiers engaged in honorable warfare. And I shall take any means within my power to rid the Country of your murderous Gang.

Earnestly yours,

J.M. Williams
Col 1ˢᵗ KS Col Vols

Williams's choice of words was ironic in light of the plundering and theft from civilians his men had committed in Jasper County in the week prior to this letter. The week following this letter saw Livingston and Union major Eno's men clashing in Jasper County, along Center Creek just west of Minersville. Williams was challenging a fight, but Livingston just vanished after the six-day running fight with Major Eno. On May 18, 1863, having received no reply to the May 11 letter, Williams ordered a smaller foraging party of the First Kansas Colored back into Jasper County on a second foraging detail. Again this was impetuous on Williams's part, as many of the men in the foraging party were unarmed.

The same day, Livingston's scouts reported sixty soldiers from the First Kansas foraging near Sherwood. Livingston led sixty-seven of his "best mounted men" to engage the Federal troops. Reports indicate between twenty-two and thirty-two African American troops of the First Kansas Colored Infantry and twenty to twenty-two white artillerymen from the Second Kansas Battery were at the home of Mrs. Rader. Mrs. Rader's husband was an officer in the Confederate army and away in service, and her son was one of Livingston's men. The Rader Farm was also a significant target from a psychological perspective, as the ten-room, frame farmhouse was the largest and most impressive home in western Jasper County and one of the best examples of a prosperous Confederate citizen. In other words, Williams and Ward were making a statement by raiding this particular farm, taking food stores and supplies. For some unknown reason, Williams sent a far smaller force than he had on the first foraging mission twelve days earlier. A mere twenty-five men of the First Kansas and twenty men of the Second Kansas Battery were with Ward now.

It seems Ward made a point of announcing his arrival to provoke an encounter with Livingston, rather than gathering supplies. The men of the First Kansas were riding in wagons and armed with muskets only. The Second Kansas were the only mounted Union troops and carried revolvers only. It is uncertain whether the teamsters driving the wagons were armed at all. This small column marched through Sherwood, stopping at the Hyden home, whose owner was fighting with Livingston. The Second Kansas rode ahead, leaving the wagons and First Kansas men at the Hyden farm. A group of ninety-seven of Livingston's men rode up to the bottom of the hill but remained out of shooting range and then rode off. Regrouping, the Union troops rode on, passing the homes of more of Livingston's men, including the Vivion home. Mrs. Vivion observed the black soldiers riding in the wagons, headed toward the Rader Farm, and had her daughter Eliza ride out to relay this information to Livingston.

Livingston had just spent six days frustrating Major Eno, who had led a force of 185 well-armed Missouri Militia cavalrymen against Livingston but failed to scatter Livingston's unit. Now, Major Ward had just 45 men at the Rader Farm, where he found a large supply of corn hidden in the upstairs rooms of the farmhouse. Ward took the precautions of setting pickets and driving Mrs. Rader and her daughters off of her property, instead of the normal practice of confiscating supplies while the women stood watching. A wagon was brought to the south side of the house, and a lieutenant called for 20 of the black soldiers to leave their muskets along the fence and to throw the corn and valuables in the house out of the second-story windows and into the wagon.

One of the white Union soldiers, Hugh Thompson, the same one who days before had received a verbal threat from the local ladies who rode into the column that Livingston would hang him, sought out Captain

Civil War rifles stacked in camp at the ready but useless if the soldiers are not close by, as was the fate of the First Kansas at the Rader Farm. Reenactment photo. *Courtesy of L. Edward Martin.*

Armstrong and Major Ward, who were at the pickets. His horse had been injured, and he sought permission to switch horses. Receiving word that Thompson needed to speak with them, Armstrong and Ward returned to the farmhouse. Before they or Thompson could begin speaking, shooting broke out behind them. Livingston's men had cut off the six men on picket duty and were able to surprise the Federal troops at the Rader farmhouse. Three Union soldiers were killed within minutes, and another three white soldiers and two black soldiers were captured. Two white soldiers and the black soldiers were still in the house when the shooting started. Running outside, the white men escaped but the black men were shot down "before taking a dozen steps."

Hugh Thompson was shot from his horse and received four or five gunshot wounds. Hitting the ground, Thompson saw Livingston riding close by and took a shot, hitting Livingston in the hand. Thompson then took aim for Livingston head's but was stopped by Richard Twitty, who dismounted and kicked Thompson in the stomach. Twitty closed in on Thompson, who was pleading that he was dying, so Twitty instead mounted and rode away. Thompson was able to reach cover of timber. After a quarter mile, he ran into two of the black soldiers who had escaped. They assisted Thompson, but Thompson's injuries were too serious for him to go on. Giving them his revolver, he told the black soldiers to go on without him because the rangers would be looking for them. Thompson took refuge in the brush of a fallen tree and listened to Livingston's men call to one another well into the night, looking for the Union soldiers.

Thompson was discovered the next morning by Thomas Crowell, a fourteen-year-old local boy. He took Thompson to his house and rode to Baxter Springs to inform Colonel Williams of Thompson's whereabouts. A detail was sent from Baxter Springs to retrieve Thompson, who survived his wounds to give a firsthand account of the Rader Farm Massacre. After the battle, Mrs. Vivion saw one Union wagon with two men racing back toward her house and called out, asking of the rest of the Union soldiers. One man yelled back, "Shot to hell!" Mrs. Rader packed a wagon and took her daughters south to Texas that evening. Her husband was later killed in battle. The Rader family never returned to Missouri.

Horses and mules were as valuable as guns and artillery in the field. Relieving the enemy of their animals was an effective guerrilla tactic. Reenactment photo. *Courtesy of L. Edward Martin.*

Livingston's report to General Sterling Price reads:

> On the 18*th*, my scouts reported 60 negroes and white men, belonging to Colonel Williams negro regiment, with five six-mule teams [wagons], foraging on Centre Creek Prairie. I ordered out 67 of my best-mounted men. I came upon them at Mrs. Rad[e]r's, pillaging her premises. I afterward learned that they were ordered not to take more plunder than they could take with them. I charged them at the house, flanking them on the right, routed them, and pursued them about 8 miles, to the crossing of Spring River. The enemy's loss in killed was, negroes 23, and 7 white men, wounded, unknown; and prisoners: also captured 30 mules and five wagons; a box containing 1,400 cartridges and caps, a good many guns, pistols &...I sustained no loss.

Lieutenant Smith of the Second Kansas reported three of his men being killed but made no mention of the First Kansas's casualties.

Williams learned of the battle at Rader's farm late in the day and ordered out five companies and some cavalry, almost four hundred men. They marched from Baxter Springs through the night, reaching Sherwood at daylight. Some of Livingston's men were spotted at a distance near Sherwood but were not within range to engage. When the Union men reached the Rader Farm, they found the bodies of the black soldiers where they had fallen the day before. They gathered the bodies they could find, eleven in all, and placed them in the house, preparing to set it on fire.

Delaying the order, Williams made another inflammatory move at this point. En route from Baxter Springs, Williams and his men came upon John Bishop. Bishop, forty-seven years old, was one of Livingston's men who had been taken prisoner in the autumn of 1862. He had been released a couple of days before from Fort Lincoln, twelve miles north of Fort Scott and approximately seventy-five miles from the Sherwood area, and was walking home in a pair of U.S. government–issue shoes. Unfortunately for Bishop, some of Williams's men recognized him and told Williams that he had been found near the scene of the massacre with a weapon. Williams had Bishop marched into the Rader farmhouse and shot, and his body was thrown on top of those of the black soldiers. Williams later wrote of Bishop, "I felt it to be my duty to shoot him on the spot and he was accordingly summarily executed."

Residents looked on as the troops prepare to set the Rader House on fire, along with the bodies of dead black Union soldiers and the executed John Bishop. Reenactment photo. *Courtesy of L. Edward Martin.*

Williams then had the Rader farmhouse torched in full view of the residents of Sherwood and ordered that "everything in a five-mile radius be burned." At least twelve farms were burned, and the entire town of Sherwood, population of 250 and the leading commercial center left in Jasper County, was burned to the ground, never to be rebuilt. Where there were families living in houses, the occupants were given a few minutes to grab what possessions they could carry before the house was set on fire. Mrs. Vivion and her daughter Eliza were among those who hurriedly packed some possessions into a wagon and headed south to Texas, as had Mrs. Rader the night before.

Williams's decision to burn the bodies of his soldiers is shrouded in controversy. It was not the policy of the Union to burn its dead soldiers; rather, it was to dig mass graves when a large number of soldiers were killed and their bodies could not be returned to a post. Williams and some of his men later claimed they felt it was necessary because they didn't have time to dig graves or return the bodies to Fort Blair at Baxter Springs due to the danger of another attack by Livingston. This explanation seems hollow considering that Williams took time to burn farms and an entire town, including allowing residents to first remove belongings. Moreover, the bodies of the white soldiers who died at the Rader Farm were not burned. The

Rader Farm battle was the worst loss to a black unit up to that point in the war, in all theaters.

If Williams had planned on provoking a response with his foraging parties, it was his men who suffered the consequences. He sent in troops who were not highly experienced against a much larger, better-armed foe with extensive experience. Additionally, the highly visible manner in which he sent them into the area, where some undoubtedly would be recognized as former slaves, was not in the interest of his men. Unfortunately, there was an emotional impact from his orders. The black soldiers who died at the Rader Farm suffered a level of brutality not often seen, even in such a brutal war. Did the scene Williams found contribute to his imprudent decision to burn the bodies of his men? Williams described the scene:

> *I visited the scene of the engagement the morning after its occurrence. And for the first time beheld the horrible evidences of the demoniac spirit of these rebel fiends in their treatment of our dead and wounded. Men were found with their brains beaten out with clubs, and the bloody weapons left at their sides, and their bodies most horribly mutilated.*

Williams's writings after the war indicate that some of the participants on the Confederate side at Rader Farm were actually residents of the area or men who were not part of Livingston's unit. It is unknown whether these brutal acts of desecration were deeds of Livingston's men or the local residents.

The burning of the Rader Farm and of Sherwood would ultimately play out national politics and strategy in western Jasper County, Missouri. The Union had only begun using black troops in combat the previous fall, and the official Confederate response was to proclaim that black soldiers would not be viewed as enemy soldiers or prisoners of war but rather escaped slaves, implying that they could be summarily killed or pressed into slavery. President Lincoln had replied by ordering that should Union soldiers not be given proper treatment as soldiers and prisoners of war, the Union would respond in like and equivalent treatment of Confederate soldiers—in essence an eye for an eye policy, which was felt necessary to prevent atrocities to black soldiers.

Williams received his response the following day, in the form of the following letter from Thomas Livingston:

Camp Jackson May 20th 1863
Col Williams, honored sir
I have five of your Sol[di]ers prisoners three Whi[te] and two Black men.
The whi[te] men I propose exchanging with you if you have any of My
men or other confederate Sol[di]ers to exchange for Them. [A]s for the
Negros I cannot recognize them as Sol[di]ers and, in cons[e]quence I will
hav[e] to hold them as contrabands of war. [I]f my proposal S[ui]tes your
will, return immediately my men or other Confederate sol[di]ers and I will
send you your men. You arrested a citizen of this neighborhood by the name
of Bishop. If that is your mode of warfare to arrest civil citizens who are
living at home and trying to raise a crop for their families, let me know and
I will try to play to your hand. Mr. Bishop was once arrested, taken to Fort
Scott examined, released and passed home a civil citizen. Some of your men
stated that he was burnt up in Mrs. Rader's house, but I am satisfied that
you are too high-toned a gentleman to stoop, or condescend to such brutal
deeds of barbarity.

I remain yours truly,
T.R. Livingston Maj comdg confederate forces [1st Missouri Cavalry Battalion]

Williams's reply, softer in tone than his initial letter, still has a patronizing overtone:

Head Quarters 1st K.C.V. Camp Hooker Ks. May 21st 1863
Maj T.R Livingston, Commanding Confederate forces
Sir Yours of the 20th is at hand. You have in your custody as I believe
Privates, Pipkins & Whitstine of the 2nd Kansas Battery for which I will
exchange two confederate Soldiers, now prisoners in my camp. In regard to
the other white man now a prisoner with you, I do not know of any man
belonging to my command not otherwise accounted for. And you can arrange
for his exchange at Fort Scott. In regard to the colored men, prisoners,
belonging to my Regiment, I have this to say, that it rests with you to treat
them as prisoners of war or not but be assured that I shall keep a like
number of your men as prisoners until these colored men are accounted for,
and you can safely trust that I shall visit a retributive justice upon them for
any injury done them at the hands of the confederate forces, and if twenty
days are allowed to pass without hearing of their exchange I shall conclude

that they have been murdered by your Soldiers or shared a worse fate by being sent in chains to the slave pens of the South, and they will be presumed to be dead. In regard to Bishop I have to say that he was known as a paroled prisoner of war, he was taken in arms against our forces, and was convicted of having shot a wounded prisoner, disarmed and at his mercy, he was shot and shared the fate of other Soldiers for whom spades could not be found to dig their graves, and if this be "brutal barbarity" compare it to the fiendish treatment he himself visited upon one of my men and of the bodies of club bruised, and brain bespattered corpses of my men left on the prairie by your men and leave it to a candid world who profits by the comparisons, Sir these men are enlisted and sworn into the service of the United States as soldiers,

A dispatch is delivered to the Southern commander. Communication and orders were delivered by messengers as well as by local residents sometimes. Reenactment photo. *Courtesy of Alex Martin.*

and I doubt not the Government I have the honor to serve will take necessary steps to punish her enemies amply for any such gross violation of all rules of civilized and honorable warfare, and you can rest assured that knowing the justice of the course, I shall not long wait for orders in the premises, but will act as I have a right to upon my own judgment, and myself assume the responsibility and if you take exceptions to this course of procedure you are at liberty to "play to my hand" as best suit your pleasure or convenience, "But I will promise to follow suit or trump" If these two men appear in Camp Pipkins and Whitstine unharmed by your forces, I will conduct beyond my lines two Soldiers of the confederate army in exchange for them, you will of course furnish them with exchange papers, And your men will be furnished accordingly, or if you choose to send a man with them, he will be allowed to return with the men exchanged for.

J.M. Williams Col Commanding Regt.

The exchange continued as Livingston replied two days later:

Chester Mo May 23rd [1863]

Col Williams.

Sir, I send you Wheley H. Pipkins and David Whitstine, which you will please send me two Confederate Soldiers in return for them. I have yet in my custody a private soldier by the name of W.T. Akers belonging to the 6th Kansas. If it suits your views you can send me a man for him, for which I will send him to you, as soon as I receive my man; I have a better opinion of your Government in regard to the treatment of prisoners and citizens than you appear to have from the tenor of your letter. For they very well know that my Government is very able to retaliate, and have it in their power to do so at least three to one, though they do not allow such conduct. I understand that you have a Confederate Soldier in your hands that is somewhat crippled. If it suits you, you can send him for one as I want you to have able bodied men in your possession.

TR Livingston, Major Com of Batt. Bloody Spikes

Ward made an immediate reply in Williams's place:

Head Quarters 1st [Kansas Colored Volunteer Infantry] *Camp Hooker* [Kansas] *May 23 1863*

Maj T.R. Livingston

Sir, Yours of this date is at hand and contents noted. The two men sent by you for Exchange Pipkins and Whitstine having arrived safely in Camp, I released your [Tenithus] Jacobs and S.Y. Shirir and will give them a safe pass through the lines. As to the prisoner Akers held by you, the proper place to exchange him will be at Fort Scott. Yours Respectfully,

R. [Richard] *G. Ward Maj 1ˢᵗ K.C.V. Comdg Regiment,*

Head Quarters Camp Ben Butler

A black soldier being held prisoner by Livingston was killed in camp. Livingston contended that a man who came in camp, not belonging to his unit, killed the Union soldier. Williams was holding Livingston responsible and later wrote that he and Livingston met face to face to negotiate over this issue but that he was not satisfied by Livingston's version of the events. Williams continued the debate in his next letter:

May 26ᵗʰ 1863

Maj T.R. Livingston

Sir, I desire to call your attention to the fact that one of the colored prisoners in your Camp was murdered by your soldiers. And I therefore demand of you the body of the man who committed the dastardly act. And if you fail to comply with the demand, and do not within forty eight hours, deliver to me this assassin, shall hang one of the men who are now prisoners in my camp. Further, you must understand that when I burn a dwelling in a Rebel country, it is a notice to the occupants thereof to remove beyond the Federal lines, and failing to do which, they will be summarily dealt with, and if afterwards found quartered upon any Union mans premises they will be treated as thieves and marauders, and neither age nor sex shall shield them from the full measure of punishment due to such criminals. I enclose herewith a copy of a letter from Gen [James G.] Blunt, to one Col Parker and I feel myself bound by its directions, and fully competent to execute the same. I repeat to you that I am not going to lie here hunting a rebel force, who have no specific character or purpose and who are supported by persons living within our lines. Tell them from me to put their house in order, for if I cannot find the force and have a fair stand up fight, I will destroy them by taking from them the means whereby they live.

Yours &c JM Williams Col Comdg

P.S. You need not excuse the murder of the colored man by claiming that it was beyond your power to prevent it. If you are fit to command, you can control your men, and I shall act from the belief that the murder was committed by your consent and will receive no excuse therefore.

The challenge of words was met with a quick retort by Livingston:

May 27ᵗʰ 1863 Col Williams
Sir yours of the 26ᵗʰ is at hand and contents noted. I confess my surprise at an Officer of your rank should have fixed such conditions to your demand as you are doubtless aware that the one who committed the offense charged is not a member of any company over which I have any control but was casually at my camp & became suddenly enraged and an altercation took place between him and Deceased which resulted in a way I very much regret & that said offender's whereabouts is to me unknown, consequently, making it impossible for me to comply with your demand, and as to threats of retaliation upon prisoners of mine that you hold. I am not aware that you have any belonging to my command. Consequently the innocent will have to suffer for the guilty and I much regret that you compel me to adopt your own rule, but had much rather be governed by the established usage of civilized warfare Sir your letter with accompanying letters from Gen [James G.] Blunt, will be immediately laid before the Government of the Confederate States unless immediately retracted by you and your answer will be anxiously looked for. In regard to your threats against both sexes carries with it its own consideration and needs no reply to. In regard to the little attack made upon your train yesterday, it was by some forces on their way to my command. If I had been there myself or some of my old trained Spikes, it would have been a sure thing though I hope you will meet before long and then I will show you how I can shuffle the cards. I have the honor to remain your most obedient
T.R. Livingston Major Com. Confederate forces

Livingston later took an opportunity to taunt Williams in similar fashion:

Camp Lonely June 8ᵗʰ 1863.
Col Williams
Sir I visited your lonely camp on yesterday, captured two prisoners viz: Corporal Larkin and Private James Martin, both belonging to Captain

Many units lived off the land for extended periods of time. It was common for headquarters to be in thick wooded areas for concealment. Reenactment photo. *Courtesy of Alex Martin.*

Smith's Artillery [2nd Independent Battery, Kansas Light Artillery]. *Likewise captured one of your beef contractors, David Harlan, on his return from your camp. I am not disposed to treat him even he being your beef contractor, as you had an inoffensive neighbor of mine treated* [Bishop] *that is killed and burned. I propose exchanging him for a prisoner you have in your camp, Paddy Scott. If the exchange suits you, as soon as you forward one Scott I will release Harlan. I would love for the business to be hastened as much as possible, lest Harlan should imitate the example of Powers when in our hands and meet the same unfortunate fate as a penalty for attempting to escape. In regard to the other two prisoners I wish to exchange them for some prisoners at Fort Scott or Springfield. If the matter can be arranged through you, you will notify me of the fact.*

I have the honor, Colonel to remain Yours Most Obedient

Major T.R. Livingston. Comdg confederate forces

P.S. On yesterday I had a sure thing and I hope that in a few days I will have another Yours T.R.L.

Williams replied the same day:

Hd. Qrs. Camp Ben Butler June 8th 1863

Maj. T.R. Livingston

Sir I am in receipt of you communication of the 8th inst, and in reply, will say that you can effect the exchange of Corp'l Larkin and Private Martin as you request by sending them to this camp or to Fort Scott, to Maj Blair Comd'g that Post. In regard to Harlan, I have this to say, he does not in any way belong to the service, and was in my camp yesterday by my order, and through threats, with some beef, and cannot even be considered a contractor but was a citizen of the Cherokee Nation who has in no way done Service for the United States, but has been taken prisoner by the United States, and released on parole; and is looked upon with suspicion by our forces, and if you injure him you will do as great an injury to your service as to ours. Consequently he cannot be treated as a prisoner of war, unless taken in arms. Bishop was a paroled prisoner of war, not exchanged, and being again captured in arms against our forces, suffered a proper penalty as other paroled men in your command will be treated if captured. If it be your policy to take prisoners, everybody you meet without reference to his acts, I can say that it is a game that both sides can play at, and I will promise to try and keep even with you.

Respectfully Yours

J.W. Williams, Col Comd'g

P.S. You speak of "sure things" which means I find a chance for your whole force to engage 3 men, now if your men want a sure thing of honor I will send an equal force to meet yours in a hand to hand fight and let the result prove who are the best men, or on whom fortune smiles.

J.M. Williams

One last letter was sent by Livingston:

Hd Qrs Camp Ben Butler

June 13th 1863

Col Williams

Sir yours of the 8th is at hand and contents noted. As the proposals of my first not did not suit you, I have not others to make. If you had sent me the prisoner that I called for in exchange for Harlen we would then have proceeded as I proposed. As your party is owing me some forty-two prisoners by my trusting to their honor, but finding that had not leaving themselves, therefore in my debt. I shall hereafter adopt a cash system with you. Here is one and there is the other. Coincidentally, if my first note is not complied with by tomorrow evening, I shall turn those prisoners over to Col Stan [Stand] *Watie* [Indian Cavalry Brigade] *with orders to forward them to Little Rock, where you can arrange matters to suit you with my superiors. In regard to your fair and honorable fight you speak of, I would suppose that men of your stripe would call it honorable for white men and gentlemen to equalize themselves to come out hand-to-hand against a lot of Ethiopians commanded by a lot of low-down thieving white men. Such honor & laurels as that I do not wish to be the garner but you hold fast to your post, and I will sure give you a fight that I call honorable. In regard to Bishop being a paroled soldier or otherwise being captured with arms, either you or your informant setting forth that base falsehood. I have Maj* [Benjamin S.] *Henning* [Third Wisconsin Cavalry] *letters on Bishop's release, and likewise, living witnesses that saw him when captured by you to prove my statement.*

Respectfully yours,

TR Livingston Commanding the Bloody Spikes

Williams made good on his promise to execute a prisoner in response to the death of the black soldier in Livingston's camp. One of Livingston's men being held as a prisoner at Fort Lincoln, twelve miles north of Fort Scott, was marched outside of the fort and summarily shot. These events marked the first occasion when the respective policy to respond in kind when black soldiers were not afforded the conventions of prisoner of war status.

Livingston moved into Indian Territory then, and records from Union units in Indian Territory make clear he had been seen in the area early in July. However, for an unclear reason, Livingston then appeared farther north and east in southwest Missouri than he had ever operated. Livingston and his men attacked a small group of Missouri Militia at Stockton, Missouri, on July 11, 1863. During the engagement, Livingston was shot next to the

BATTLE OF RADER'S FARM
MAY 18, 1863

IN MEMORY OF 18
U. S. SOLDIERS KILLED IN
ACTION 3 MILES NORTH
OF THIS PARK.

Monument regarding the Battle of Rader's Farm, situated in Schifferdecker Park, Joplin, Missouri. *Courtesy of L. Edward Martin.*

courthouse while leading the assault. He fell from his horse, and as Livingston tried to rise, several Union soldiers emerged from the courthouse. One of the Union solders picked up Livingston's pistol and struck him with a "horrific" blow to the head. Several others fired into his body. Livingston's body and those of two of his men were left on the courthouse lawn as Livingston's men retreated. Livingston is said to be buried in an unmarked grave in the cemetery at Stockton, Missouri.

A couple of days later, one of Livingston's men, Tom Webb, returned to Stockton and was able to retrieve two of the three dead men, with speculation that one of those bodies was that of Thomas Livingston. Various sources indicate that Webb returned to Jasper County and buried the men on his property, which was situated just north of that of Solomon Rothanbarger. A week later, Union troops rode onto Webb's farm and walked him and his teenage son, Austin, into the woods, where they shot them in the back of the heads. Webb's wife and younger son found the bodies, and the boy went to Rothanbarger, who returned with a wagon and helped the boy bury his father and brother. Later, the two Webbs were reinterred in the Webb City cemetery. In September 1863, two months later, Jo Shelby made a raid into Missouri. Riding on Stockton, the citizens were panicked, assuming Shelby would destroy the town. Shelby and his men rode to the center of town, burned the courthouse and rode on, leaving the rest of Stockton unmolested.

People shied away from the site of the burnt Rader farmhouse and the memories of the burned men. Stories of the site being haunted by the ghosts of the men who died there spread. About twenty years after the war, ignoring the legends, a family moved onto the land and built a house on the foundation of the Rader house. They lived there and farmed successfully until some fifty years later, when the house mysteriously burned. The family decided not to rebuild, and the site of the Rader house was never built upon again. Other buildings have been built nearby, including a now old, dilapidated school building owned by the county that is continually the site of odd happenings, generally blamed on trespassers and kids. The locked door stands open repeatedly, and the entrance shows signs of scorching and smoke damage. It may well be vandalism, but as many current residents don't know what transpired a few hundred yards away, one wonders if the culprits will be found.

Sherwood was not rebuilt and became private property. Having visited the site with permission of the current owners, it still has an eerie feel to the place, with a foreboding feeling. In the springtime, you can see the lines of irises and other bulb plants sprout and bloom in neat tidy lines, outlining where homes stood 150 years ago, now shielded by timber. The cemetery is overgrown and neglected. You feel a sadness as you walk through the many tombstones, many so worn to be illegible or broken, sinking into the ground.

While standing near some of the oldest tombstones, I and another female member of Paranormal Science Lab heard a man's voice, soft and indistinct. We turned and confirmed that we were alone. One stone in particular is interesting in that it has only a roughly carved symbol, roughly approximating an L shape. In the late 1880s, the farmer whose land surrounds the cemetery observed an old man drive to the cemetery in a rickety one-horse carriage and place the stone. The farmer assumed it was a grave from years before or perhaps was to be the old man's own grave. The farmer watched the old man over several months strain with a hammer and chisel, carving on the stone. The man would break down crying. Eventually, the old man stopped coming to the cemetery, and no funeral occurred. It is unknown who, if anyone, is buried in that grave. Stories have circulated that Thomas Livingston is buried in the grave and the symbol is in fact an L. Some local legends claim that some of Livingston's men would meet at the grave to give their respects to their old leader. This is interesting, as there are similar stories that his men would risk detection, which would have been dangerous for some years after the war, and gather at the unmarked grave of Livingston in the Stockton cemetery.

The oldest cemetery in western Jasper County is Peace Church Cemetery, which lies a mere quarter mile from the Rader Farm. There have been claims of ghosts and paranormal activity at Peace Church Cemetery for years. Most such activity is credited to the fact that the infamous serial killer Billy Cook is buried there. Cook grew up in Joplin, abandoned along with his siblings by a drunkard father after their mother died. Billy did not fare well at the hands of his foster mother, a woman who was cruel to him, in part due to a birth defect that left Billy unable to close one eyelid. Billy ended up in prison as a teenager and, after being released, started hitchhiking and went on a killing spree, which became the basis for the 1950s film noir classic *The Hitchhiker*. After Billy's execution at age twenty-one, one of his sisters paid to have him buried in Peace Church Cemetery under cover of darkness. His grave was later moved outside the wall of the original cemetery. Cook has become a focus of local occult interest. I have observed shadow people in the cemetery, and many who go there experience feelings of being watched and feeling uncomfortable. What few people know is that there are a number of unmarked graves of Civil War soldiers killed in the area buried in both the Peace Church Cemetery and the old Sherwood cemetery.

Likewise, the Webb City Cemetery, where Tom and Austin Webb were reinterred, is an old cemetery as well. For years, it has been said to be the site of mysterious lights that float among tombstones, particularly the areas with the oldest graves. Could these lights be the spirits of Tom Webb and his son, shot in the back in cold blood?

The Hornet Spooklight is the most infamous site of paranormal activity in southwest Missouri. South of Joplin, Missouri, in the area of the former hamlet of Hornet, is what is commonly referred to as Spooklight Road, a county road in Newton County that runs into Oklahoma to the west. Legends of the Spooklight have appeared in print since shortly after the Civil War. It appears to be an earthlight, similar to those seen in other parts of the world. The light will appear as a ball of luminescent light, free floating and seeming to bounce in the area a few feet above the roadway, in the trees along the road and in adjacent fields. It has been observed for over one hundred years.

The legends are divided between the light being either the ghosts of young Indian lovers searching for each other after they killed themselves when the chief refused permission for them to marry and that of a Civil War soldier killed in fighting, searching for his unit. Slight variations are heard as well.

Research has been conducted to explain the light, but results have been less than explanatory. One theory is that the light is actually headlights from I-44 several miles away. However, the light was observed decades before the

Thomas R. Livingston, Southwest Missouri Guerrilla Leader

Photograph of Spooklight Road. *Courtesy of Paranormal Science Lab, Lisa Livingston-Martin, photographer.*

road was there or cars had been invented. Another theory is that the light is a natural phenomenon, swamp gas, caused by luminous gases rising from decaying organic matter. But the land is not swampy, and such gases have not been found in the area.

I have witnessed the Hornet Spooklight on multiple occasions over twenty-odd years. I have no idea what the light is, but it appears to have unique properties. It can split into multiple balls of light, and on one occasion when I was with several people, we had divided to two groups, each standing a couple of hundred yards from the other and facing each other. The light appeared between the two groups. Everyone in my group could see the light, about 75 yards in front us. The other group, on seeing our reaction to the light, started walking toward us. As they neared, someone in our group called out asking if they saw the light. "Where?" was the reply, and they kept walking until they were within a few feet of the light, which then abruptly disappeared. Joining us, the other group confirmed that they never saw the light—it was viewed from one direction only.

BUSHWHACKERS BEWARE

Avilla, some six miles east of Carthage, was founded in the 1850s by, among others, Dr. Jaquillin Stemmons and his family. As slavery became a political issue, Stemmons represented those slaveholders in the region who held fast to their loyalty to the Union and did not see owning slaves as a basis for secession or rebellion. As war approached, Stemmons formed a military company for the Union. He freed his slaves, as he felt that was the best means of protecting them and ensuring their survival in the coming war. Most decided to stay with the Stemmons family despite their freeman status, and years later, several of the former slaves described Dr. Stemmons as a kind man and father figure whose surname they willingly took for their own. The Stemmons family ended up divided, with one of the doctor's sons fighting for the Confederacy. Dr. Stemmons was shot to death on March 8, 1862, by Confederate bushwhackers during a raid, when his home was also burned.

The attack on the Stemmons home was intended to intimidate Stemmons and other Union men from opposing the Confederate cause in southwest Missouri. Instead, Avilla townsmen decided to approach the bushwhackers from an offensive posture rather than the defensive stance relied upon up to that point. The citizens in Avilla took up arms. The Union army gained possession of Missouri in 1862, but the region remained overrun with bushwhackers and occasionally small bands of Confederate regulars or guerrilla raiders on horseback. It was estimated that at any given time the area between Nevada—

about sixty miles north of Carthage—and the Arkansas state line at the south end of McDonald County, Missouri, some fifty miles south of Carthage would contain up to one thousand guerrillas and bushwhackers. The Avilla town militia became a prototype for the future county militias. The patrol areas were extended within eastern Jasper and western Lawrence Counties. Patrols of mounted militiamen were augmented by a few Union soldiers of the U.S. Cavalry from Fort Scott, Kansas, and continued to protect the town and countryside in local skirmishes. The militia gained a reputation for tracking down and shooting bushwhackers, who came to fear the Avilla pioneer marksmen. In one account, a Rebel's skeleton was found just south of town with a bullet hole in the skull; his name was never identified. He had apparently been killed during a previous skirmish with militiamen, but his remains were not found until they were in an advanced state of decomposition. The skull was then hung from the "Death Tree" in Avilla, suspended from a tree limb for over a year near the road at the Dunlap apple orchard, now abandoned and defunct, as a warning to all other bushwhackers. Some accounts have the tree being an Osage orange or hedge tree that appeared dead. Some accounts say the tree was an apple tree and then stopped producing fruit, and that black crows took up a continual perch in the dead branches.

By 1863, Avilla was a Union army garrison manned by the Enrolled Missouri Militia, and the new soldiers stationed in Avilla were under the command of Major Morgan. Tents were erected and storehouses, barns and homes were converted to temporary army barracks and headquarters that housed hundreds of soldiers at various times and a number of refugees. The town became known to the Missouri Militiamen informally as "Camp Avilla," and by 1864, many of the original town militiamen continued to assist the new Missouri Militia, functioning as patrol leaders in the newly organized Jasper County Militia. Avilla supported anti-guerrilla operations in the region while under Lieutenant Colonel T.T. Crittenden of the Missouri State Militia's Seventh Cavalry and facilitated as a way station when needed in the transportation of Confederate prisoners of war. Being situated in open grassland, Avilla was able to maintain a formidable and effective defense and became a sanctuary for refugees of nearby burned-out towns such as Carthage. But the area remained dangerous until the end and even for some time after the war.

Avilla today is a quiet hamlet along Highway 96 (old Route 66). There are abandoned commercial buildings as well as active businesses. Not much from the Civil War years remains, but the streets are laid out much as they

The Avilla Post Office. Shadow people are said to walk through the locked doors. *Courtesy of the author.*

were during the war. There are legends of various shadow people being seen along the main street and businesses. Shadow people are thought to be paranormal entities that appear as a dark shadow form in a general human shape; most appear featureless. Some have been said to appear in the old park just north of the highway, standing under abandoned store awnings, in windows and even walking through the locked doors of the U.S. Post Office (old Avilla Bank Building).

These shadow entities may be residual in nature, meaning that they are an imprint on the environment and replay events from the past. One shadow person in Avilla has been called "Otis" by some in reference to the town drunk character on the *Andy Griffith Show*, as it seems to stumble from the old tavern building and allegedly has been seen lying down on the road. Residual hauntings are theorized to occur due to extreme emotion—anything from extreme elation to extreme terror or sadness—experienced in a location. The experience of the residents of the area during the Civil War certainly has the potential of imprinting emotion in this location, if imprinting is possible. While the old tavern and post office were not built at the time of the war, there were structures in these areas, so it may be possible that these shadow people are reliving events that occurred on site but in different physical structures.

Could it be that the drunken behavior observed of the shadow person called Otis could perhaps be of a man shot and stumbling out of a house or other structure and falling down, rather than passing out from intoxication?

It is said by witnesses that the shadow people are most easily observed with peripheral vision and can appear during daytime sunlight or at night but seem most common during late nighttime and early morning hours with moonlight, especially if snow is on the ground. Presumably, the white background provides relief so that one can see a shadow in limited light. It is also said that the shadows do not appear threatening or cause fear and have not interfered with the living.

A ghost tale in Avilla that seems most directly connected to events of the Civil War is that of the Avilla Specter or Avilla Phantom, which has grown out of the story of the bushwhacker skull hanging in the Avilla Death Tree. This phantasm is reputed to be aware or interested in the living who stray past and takes interest in scaring the unwary passerby. If true, this could be a different type of entity, perhaps the kind of ghost that returns to torment the living or a revenant or some type of interactive, or intelligent, ghost, as it appears aware of what is happening and behaves in a manner that could be intended to frighten witnesses. Witnesses have described him as a lurking, headless shadowy figure in a long duster with an antique firearm slung on his back. The phantom bushwhacker sometimes stands with an outstretched hand as if searching for something, but he has also been seen crawling low to the ground, as if trying to avoid detection by militia patrols. The phantom is seen most often on cool autumn nights along the roads and fields surrounding Avilla. Some assume that he searches for his head or skull, which was disturbed and placed in the tree.

Many stories of haunting center on spirits who are not at rest due to an improper burial or their remains being disturbed. Local residents have dubbed the frightful ghost Rotten Johnny Reb. Witnesses have claimed to have shined a flashlight on the ghost and the beam "went through like he was transparent, before we ran away frantically." Legend has grown that if you can find the old tree from which his skull hung, under certain light you may see the image of the skull and perhaps send the Death Tree Phantom to the other side. My first impression of the legend of finding the tree was that it would be nearly impossible, as it was common for a hanging tree to be cut down to avoid bad luck befalling the area. However, it may not have been viewed as a hanging tree, as the victim was not hanged but, rather, the skull was later found and placed in the tree. There are very old trees in the area, so it is possible that the tree still stands.

The Avilla Death Tree story is not unique. A similar event occurred in Stone County, between the towns of Galena and Reeds Spring, Missouri, at a lonely spot to become known as Ghost Pond and also Dead Man's Pond. A large party of bushwhackers, numbering 120 or more, rode north out of Arkansas into southwest Missouri on the Wilderness Road. These were bushwhackers in the most pejorative meaning of the word. Their goal was theft, to rustle cattle and whatever they could find that they could take to Arkansas and make profit. The legend goes that the bushwhackers made camp at the pond and the following day rode into Galena, demanding that the citizens give them money and valuables. Three townsmen were shot, and one is said to have been hanged by the thieves. The bushwackers captured some 150 head of cattle and 50 horses, plus what loot they had taken, and started back down the Wilderness Road.

As happened at Avilla, the violence did not have the intended effect on the residents. The militia was alerted and pursued the bushwhackers through the thick woods and hills surrounding Galena. They caught up to the bushwhackers near Railey Creek. From the cover of a tree line, the militia opened fire, and more than one hundred men on each side were firing. The militia was successful in running off the livestock, and the bushwhackers fled, taking the rest of their plunder. The bushwhackers did not see the militia pursue them and made camp again at the pond.

The militia surrounded the camp in the night, killed the sentries and attacked the camp at daybreak. The bushwhackers were awakened to gunfire. A skirmish raged as the militia killed men in their blankets and as they stumbled to their feet. Of the 120 bushwhackers who rode up from Arkansas, it was said only about 20 returned, as the militia pursued men as they escaped on foot or horseback. Bodies were stacked around the pond, and 9 bodies were later pulled from the water. However, all of the bodies were not recovered, and the water turned foul, such as wildlife would not drink from it. Some years later, a farmer pulled a skull from the pond and wedged it into a tree stump nearby, where it remained for many years. Human bones, miniballs and gun parts were recovered over the years from the pond. Ghosts have been seen around the pond appearing as old bushwhackers. People shied away from the pond for many years, especially at night. There are differing accounts on the location of the pond, but many say it is the pond now called Morrill's Pond.

NEWTON COUNTY
THE CONFEDERATE CAPITAL OF MISSOURI

Neosho, Missouri, the county seat of Newton County, some twenty miles south of Carthage, became the site of the "Confederate capitol" of Missouri when the legislature and Governor Jackson met in the old Masonic Hall on October 21, 1861, and voted to formally secede from the Union. The approach of Federal troops caused the House and Senate of the state legislature to adjourn from the Masonic Hall and to reconvene ten days later in Cassville, where the ordinance of secession and act of affiliation to the Confederacy were signed. Cassville, county seat of Barry County to the east of Newton County, was attacked by one side and then the other throughout the remainder of the war. The courthouse in Cassville, as many in southwest Missouri, was turned into a makeshift fort, with a ditch dug around its perimeter and fortified and the building "portholed" to make attacks less deadly.

Neosho was a Confederate stronghold during the first years of the war, with many Confederate-sympathizing families loading up wagons and going there for protection. A refugee camp ultimately grew up around Neosho and the military camp. Conditions were deplorable; provisions were in short supply, and disease was a constant fear. It was in this refugee camp that Lucy Cox, the daughter of Judge John C. Cox of Blytheville (site of present-day Joplin, Missouri), died of disease, likely smallpox. The Cox family had abandoned their land after Major Thomas Livingston's Cherokee Spikes

Monument honoring Neosho as the site of the "Confederate capitol" of Missouri during the Civil War, on the north side of the Newton County courthouse on the square in Neosho, Missouri. *Courtesy of the author.*

had burned his house, and Lucy stopped the guerrillas from shooting her father by placing herself in front of him. The motive for burning the Cox homestead is unknown; however, Judge Cox was also prominent in mining in the area, as was Livingston. It is said that Judge Cox returned to his home with a military escort so that Lucy's body could be buried in the family cemetery. The Cox family returned and rebuilt a house on the same Blytheville property after the war.

The small hamlet of Newtonia, in Newton County, served as a Confederate post at various times during the war, in part because of its proximity to the Granby lead mines, which supplied a majority of the lead for bullets for the Confederate army. There were two battles fought in Newtonia.

The First Battle of Newtonia occurred as Confederate troops in Arkansas planned an invasion of southwest Missouri, attempting to secure the strategically important area once and for all. In September 1862, some 4,000 Confederate troops were encamped around Newtonia awaiting the arrival of reinforcements led by General Hindman, who did not follow through with the promised invasion. At the same time, approximately 6,000 Federal troops with eighteen cannons were encamped a mere twelve miles north at Sarcoxie, in Jasper County. Advance parties skirmished on September 29. The next morning, the Union force marched on Newtonia, and by 7:00 a.m., both forces were fully engaged in the fighting. The Union advance force found a larger-than-expected opponent at Newtonia and was quickly outnumbered. Some of the Indian soldiers from Cooper's Choctaw and Chickasaw Mounted Rifles Regiment raced down Main Street letting out piercing battle cries. The Federal line broke and ran, pursued for more than six hours until they met up with the main Union force. The Union commander, Brigadier General Frederick Salomon, regrouped his men and assaulted the defensive positions at Newtonia unsuccessfully, including the long stone wall on the Ritchey farm. Federal losses were 50 killed, 80 wounded and 115 missing, while the Confederate losses were 12 killed, 63 wounded and 3 missing. Ritchey family accounts describe the front lawn littered with cannonballs when they returned home after the battle. The Confederates could not celebrate the victory, as four days later, Union General John Schofield amassed 18,000 troops with fifty-two pieces of artillery in southwest Missouri and marched into Newtonia, forcing the Confederates to retreat into Arkansas. The region was effectively in Union hands for the rest of the war; however, guerrilla units continued to be a serious threat to Federal troops and supply movements in the region.

The Second Battle of Newtonia, the last major engagement in southwest Missouri, occurred in late 1864. General Sterling Price, always devoted to

Infantry with rifles were invaluable and could inflict considerable damage in skilled hands. Reenactment photo. *Courtesy of Alex Martin.*

his home state of Missouri, had been requesting permission for a major invasion of Missouri for two years. In August 1864, he received approval and advanced into Missouri with twelve thousand underequipped men. The ideal targets would have been St. Louis and Jefferson City, but they were too well fortified and defended for a realistic attack. Price pushed north and advanced along the Kansas-Missouri border. On October 6, 1864, the Union had received a harsh blow as General Blunt's troops were severely beaten by Price's troops at the Battle of Baxter Springs, Kansas, some fifteen miles from the western side of Jasper County, Missouri.

Price pushed north and advanced near Kansas City but was badly defeated at the Battle of Westport, Missouri, four miles from Kansas City on October 23, 1864. Price was without a choice; he had to retreat after pushing so far north of his supply lines, especially after October 25, 1864, with the Battle of Mine Creek, just over the Kansas line from Vernon County, Missouri, where over nine hundred of Price's men were captured by the Federal pursuing army.

Reenactors Steve Cottrell and Cliff Kester demonstrate steady nerves while under attack. Reenactment photo. *Courtesy of Alex Martin.*

By October 28, 1864, the Confederates were encamped just south of Newtonia when Union General Blunt saw an opportunity to redeem himself for his defeat at Baxter Springs. He was in charge of an advance force of about one thousand men when he came across some of Price's men gathering corn from a field. Outnumbered, Blunt's line was stretched thin, as he failed to wait for the main force to catch up to him before opening fire. Price ordered General Joseph Shelby to hold the Union troops off so the main Confederate force could escape south.

Shelby opened fire successfully and initially pushed Blunt back over a mile and a half. Shelby mounted a massive frontal assault on the middle of the Federal line. Blunt was able to hold the line with use of artillery. Blunt's men were running low on cartridges, and one company of the Third Wisconsin Cavalry ran out of munitions but held its line, anticipating fighting with sabers only. Blunt was saved by the timely arrival of General Curtis and a full brigade of reinforcements. Darkness was falling, and Shelby had succeeded in providing Price time to retreat. Shelby withdrew his men, and Curtis did not pursue him into nightfall. This marked the end of fighting by regular Confederate units in southwest Missouri.

The impressive Ritchey Mansion, built in 1851 by Matt Ritchey, is virtually a twin to the Kendrick House in Carthage, Missouri (they shared the same contractor/builder, Thomas Dawson). It was used as a field hospital during the two battles at Newtonia, and fighting occurred on Ritchey's land, some within sight of the house. A dining table was used as an operating table in one of the upstairs bedrooms. Afterward, it became known as the "Black

The Ritchey Mansion in Newtonia, Missouri. There is still damage on the left front corner from a cannonball. The front lawn was littered with cannonballs after the First Battle of Newtonia. *Courtesy of the author.*

The "Black Room" in the Ritchey Mansion. The upstairs bedroom floor was painted black to try to cover the bloodstains left from being used as a battlefield operating room. *Courtesy of the author.*

Room," as the floor was painted black in an attempt to cover the bloodstains, which could not be removed from the wooden floor.

There is a family cemetery just a few yards west of the house. In the 1960s, a large tree was uprooted during a windstorm and fell on the cemetery, particularly over the grave of Polly Ritchey, Matt Ritchey's first wife. The house was still a private residence at the time, and the following day, one of the young sons of the owners undertook the cleanup. He spent the day cutting up the tree with a chainsaw and clearing the brush and debris with a wheelbarrow. That night it was cold, and all of the family's beds were covered in warm quilts. The next morning, the family awoke cold and without their bedcovers, with the exception of the young boy who had cleaned up the tree and returned Polly's grave to its usual tidy appearance, as his bed was covered with the quilts from all of the other beds. Was Polly saying thank you and watching over her young benefactor?

People have reported seeing apparitions around the Ritchey Mansion. One particular apparition stands out. A woman in period clothing has been seen by people outside the house standing on the second-floor porch, watching the activity in the front yard. Whether this is Polly or perhaps another member of the Ritchey family is not clear.

I was fortunate to receive a tour of the Ritchey Mansion, with my guide actually being dressed in reenactor's costume of the Missouri Militia. I had an audio recorder with me, and within 3:30 minutes of starting the tour, I recorded an EVP (electronic voice phenomenon) of a woman's voice saying "go away." Whether this request was to me and my tour guide generally or to him, due to the uniform he wore, is unclear.

There is also another cemetery very near the Ritchey Mansion, concealed in a wooded area down a narrow dirt road. If you do not know the cemetery is there, you would likely turn around at the end of the dirt road and leave without knowing you were only yards away from it. There are Civil War–era graves in the cemetery, including that of an officer who died in one of the battles at Newtonia. The first time I visited the cemetery, it was overgrown and thick with thorny vines, and most of the tombstones were obscured by the undergrowth. I have visited it also during winter months when the retreat of vegetation gives you a better view. Several people expressed feelings of heaviness or oppressiveness and the sense of being watched. I have heard that strange mists have been observed floating in the cemetery, although at this time, I can make no opinion as to the cause of the mist, which is said not to be fog.

The Ritchey Mansion and portions of the battlefield have recently been sold to the National Park Service, which has plans to make it a national battlefield site under the direction of Wilson's Creek Battlefield National Park. Newtonia will make an interesting visit for Civil War enthusiasts when it opens to the public. And if you're fortunate, you may observe more than strictly the history of the site.

THE ROTHANBARGER HOUSE
UNION MAN IN CONFEDERATE COUNTRY

S olomon Rothanbarger, an immigrant from Pennsylvania, arrived in present-day Joplin, Missouri, in 1839 at age nineteen and staked out a homestead on the banks of Turkey Creek, which one day would be in the eastern part of Joplin. In 1850, he left his wife to tend to their farm and went to California seeking fortune in the gold rush. He met with success and returned a year later with money sufficient to finance a burgeoning construction and brickworks business, which became Rothanbarger & Sons, and to build a brick "mansion." The brickworks was on the site of his Turkey Creek property, producing bricks that resembled the bricks made by Sennett Rankin in building the antebellum home that became known as Kendrick House north of Carthage. Rothanbarger House was begun in about 1851, about two years after Kendrick House. The home faces south over the low river valley below and appears large from the modern street, which runs along the east edge of the property. Approaching up the driveway and walking to the house, one realizes it is smaller than upon first impression. Although virtually identical in design to the Kendrick House—federal-style, two-story, four-room brick house—it is at least one-third smaller. There is an original addition on the rear of the house, on the east side, which is the kitchen. Upon inspection of the handmade brick, interspersed among the red brick are bricks that appear gray and glazed. While arranged in patterns, they were not intended to look this way; the glazing occurred when a brick was too close to a hot spot in the wood-fired kilns, liquefying the silica in the river clay to produce a glazing that sparkles in the sunlight.

It has long been believed that the home was finished to its present appearance in the early 1850s. However, Rothanbarger family correspondence has been found that indicates that the house was originally a one-story home and that the second story was added later, perhaps even after the Civil War. Upon examining the house for clues as to whether it has always appeared as it does today, it is not evident from the front or side walls of the house that the second story was a latter addition. However, looking at the rear wall from a distance, there appears to be a line at which the colors are slightly different, with the differences uniform enough to appear that at least clay of a different color was used in making the bricks for that portion of the wall. The reason for different clay is not known, as river clay in this area is fairly uniform in appearance and readily available onsite. While it is not certain at this point when the house was finished to its present appearance, it is clear that the home had significant contact with events of the Civil War. It was used as a field hospital on multiple occasions during fighting and skirmishes in the vicinity, reputedly by both the Federals and Confederates, housing up to thirteen wounded soldiers at once. It is unclear whether soldiers died in the home, although it is a realistic possibility.

The current owners informed me that they have been visited by Rothanbarger family descendants who related that Solomon Rothanbarger's property was utilized as a stop on the Underground Railroad. The story related by the Rothanbarger descendant was that a cave overlooking Turkey Creek and almost directly south of the home was used to hide runaway slaves on their journey to freedom. It is likely that they would have been en route to Kansas, less than fifteen miles to the west, as many Northern sympathizers in southwest Missouri migrated to Kansas to escape the violence and harsh living conditions, which grew worse as the war continued.

There is also the story of Confederate bushwhackers setting fire to the front porch in an attempt to burn the house down, a common practice in the guerrilla-style warfare employed in southwest Missouri. Scorch marks are still visible on the bricks around and above the porch, extending well above the level of the floor of the second story. It does not appear that the front wall of the home has been altered or extended upward, which would seem to indicate that if the newly discovered Rothanbarger family correspondence is correct and the second story was added sometime after the war, the scorch

The Rothanbarger House, also known as History House, overlooking Turkey Creek in northwest Joplin, Missouri. Scorch marks are visible around the porch, reputedly a result of bushwhackers setting fire to the porch. *Courtesy of the author.*

marks are from a later fire. There is no clear evidence that the story of bushwhackers setting fire to the porch is mistaken either. The owner showed me where Civil War–era musket balls had been embedded into the western outer wall of the home, including one that was still firmly embedded in the brick, but whether the musket balls are from that incident is unknown. It is also said that Jesse and Frank James hid out in the springhouse by the creek in the valley below the house. The James brothers are known to have been in the area at various times while riding with the guerrilla William Quantrill.

When Mrs. Rothanbarger died, it was in the middle of a harsh winter. The ground was frozen solid, and a grave could not be dug. This was before use of morticians, before embalming, and graves had to be dug by hand. The family had no choice but to postpone a funeral until the ground thawed. Mrs. Rothanbarger was put in the west bedroom upstairs. The windows were opened to allow the cold air in the room. It was in this manner that Mrs. Rothanbarger waited two months to be buried.

The Rothanbarger House has continued to be a private residence until the present, for about 160 years, which is very unusual for a home in southwest

The Rothanbarger House

Missouri, as so few survived the Civil War. Paranormal activity has been observed for years. The current owners have observed an apparition of a woman in nineteenth-century clothing walking through the kitchen, which has been in the same location since the house was built. An apparition of a man has been observed in the addition from the yard through windows. Upon first glance, it appeared to be a live person, startling the owner. Knocking on the back door and wall has been so loud and pronounced that it could be heard at the other end of a phone conversation. Footsteps have been heard in the hallway upstairs, and people have been startled awake in the east bedroom with the sensation that they were poked in the side by an unseen hand.

Steve Cottrell, in his book, *Haunted Ozark Battlefields*, relates an event that he witnessed at the Rothanbarger House in the 1980s, when the house was owned by another couple. After a living history event, in which Cottrell was a reenactor, some of the participants decided to conduct a séance in the dining room. Cottrell elected to retire to the parlor and eventually dozed off to sleep on the couch. He was awakened by the sound of breaking glass in the same room, followed by emotional sobbing and muttering by several participants of the séance in the dining room. Upon investigation, he discovered a round piece of glass had popped out of the side of an oil lamp sitting on the mantel. Cottrell also relates that his friends said they did see a ghost once in the house, a vaporous mist moving down a hallway.

A Civil War Haunting

PARANORMAL SCIENCE LAB INVESTIGATES KENDRICK HOUSE AND THE BATTLE OF CARTHAGE BATTLEFIELD

K endrick House is the oldest standing house in Jasper County, Missouri, at 162 years old, and one of only a few antebellum homes still standing in the county. The house was built beginning in 1849 and completed by 1856. When the house was built, there were no roads leading here. There was a trail off to the east, but here there was nothing but prairie grass and trees outlining Spring River, several hundred yards to the south. Sennett Rankin was drawn to this spot in the mid-1840s, building a small log cabin on the banks of the river just southeast of the house, on which he began construction but never bore his name. A prosperous farmer with large holdings in the area, Rankin broke ground on the rolling hill above the river in 1849, as slaves tended a forty-acre field carved out of the prairie by horse and man. We have no idea what plans Sennett Rankin and his wife had when they started building what later became known as the "Mansion." After a couple of years, Sennett and his wife moved back to their large farm near present-day Jasper, Missouri, some fifteen miles north, without finishing or ever living in the house.

The partially constructed future Mansion was sold to Sennett's son-in-law, Thomas Dawson, who continued work on the house. Soon, the lure of gold took Dawson to California to seek his fortune. Dawson did not find a fortune in California, and he also didn't finish construction and never lived in the house. Perhaps as a means of recouping his losses from that search for gold, Dawson sold the still unfinished house and 540 acres of future farmland and

Kendrick House is the oldest standing home in Jasper County, Missouri, and one of only a handful of prewar homes to survive the destruction in southwest Missouri during the Civil War. *Courtesy of Paranormal Science Lab, L. Edward Martin, photographer.*

orchards to Thomas and Elizabeth Kendrick for the sizeable sum of $7,000 in 1856. At the same time in Jasper County, Missouri, land was selling for a fraction of that price. The Kendricks finished the house on the hill and made it their home. They turned the 540 acres of virgin prairie grass into cropland and orchards. The Kendrick family and their descendants, including several generations of the Janney family, lived in the home continuously for about 130 years, until it was sold to Victorian Carthage in the 1980s, which still owns the home. About 20 acres of the original 540 remain with the house.

Victorian Carthage is a nonprofit group that has as its purpose the preservation and maintenance of Kendrick Place as a living museum. Victorian Carthage restored the home in the 1980s to the appearance it would have had in the mid-1800s. Care was taken to use colors, patterns and materials that would be representative of the period. For instance, the wallpaper patterns in the home are consistent with those used in the mid-1800s. The wide-plank wood floors appear a pinkish-red in color. While they are painted with ordinary house paint today, when first built, the planks were painted with hand-mixed paint tinted with oxen blood to give it the pinkish-red color. The woodwork you see in the house is original, and most is solid walnut from

A glimpse of mid-nineteenth-century life in the parlor at Kendrick House. Reenactment photo. *Courtesy of Victorian Carthage, LLC, Kendrick House collection.*

trees felled on the property. The woodwork was hand-cut and hand-finished by carpenters laboring onsite. The limestone windowsills, as well as the limestone slabs in the fireplaces and hearths, are native limestone or Carthage marble quarried just over the hill to the west on what was originally part of Kendrick Place but later became the Carthage Marble quarry. The limestone is hard enough to be polished and in that state is referred to as Carthage Marble. It has been used for numerous buildings throughout the state and nation, including the Missouri State Capitol in Jefferson City, Missouri.

Although the city of Carthage had been established by the time Kendrick House was built, it was still a small collection of houses and buildings. There were no bridges erected in Jasper County until the 1870s, so you couldn't run to town to get lumber, nails or other building supplies. Everything used in construction of the house was either material found on the property or made by the workers. For instance, there were no store-bought nails available, so each nail was made by hand by a blacksmith in a forge. Most nails in the structure of the house are square and have very little of a head on them as a result. The outer walls are red brick, made from the clay from the banks of Spring River, just a few hundred yards from this spot. Sennett Rankin, as well as Dawson and the Kendricks, owned slaves. Rankin owned a number of slaves, and they built the outer brick walls. The bricks are concave on the interior side so as to hold more mortar. The exterior walls are three bricks thick, very unusual for construction of that time in the region, where a small log cabin with a hole cut out of one of the logs for a year-round open window was a symbol of permanence. The thickness of the walls meant that the house was better insulated than most buildings of the time. You will notice that the house is actually very quiet and you don't hear much traffic noise from outside, considering the building is 162 years old.

The house is a federal-style architecture, which means that there is an entryway and staircase with symmetrical wings on either side. Although the house looks large from the outside, the original structure consists of four rooms: dining room and parlor on either side of the entryway on the ground floor and two bedrooms on the second floor. There was no running water in the home until 1954. Water was originally available from the hand-dug well beside the house and a cistern that collected rainwater. There were various outer buildings on site, including a kitchen, slave quarters, blacksmith shop, barns and later homes for family members and rental homes for men working in the nearby quarry. The old outhouse still stands out back near the slave cabin. The original slave quarters were brick, like the house, but were demolished sometime in the past. The slave quarters on site were moved from the Miller, Missouri area when Victorian Carthage opened Kendrick House to the public.

Kendrick House drew in people even before the Civil War, as it was known as one of the finest houses in the region and a stopping point for settlers heading west, where they engaged the blacksmithing and gunsmithing services of William Kendrick and his son Joshua, as well as obtaining supplies and food for their journey. It was considered a mansion for several reasons. First, it was brick and large compared to the log cabins that were standard accommodations for the area. It was outfitted with a full complement of glass windows, which doesn't sound unusual or impressive in 2011; however, in the 1850s, glass had to be hand blown and was a luxury item and quite expensive. It also was not available locally and had to be shipped in from St. Louis, overland by ox wagon. Imagine crossing four hundred miles of natural brush, prairie and rivers without any graded roads and no bridges— all while trying to keep panes of glass from breaking. That is why houses such as Kendrick had shutters—not to keep wind or sun out but to protect the glass from breaking. A broken glass meant months until it could be replaced. As glass became more common and was available locally, the expense came down, and shutters were no longer a necessity. Compare this luxury to most early settlers, for whom a window was a hole notched out of a log in the wall of the cabin, open to the elements year-round. Most homestead cabins were one room as well. Photos of Kendrick House, taken in the 1890s, show that the shutters were in disrepair and some had fallen off the house. By that time, glass was readily available, and it didn't make sense to put money into maintaining the shutters. Hand-blown glass is made by the craftsman blowing through a glass tube, and the air then causes the molten glass to change shape. A consequence of the process was that air bubbles would form in the glass as it cooled and hardened. There are original hand-blown panes of glass in the cabinets to the side of the fireplace in the dining room. If you look closely, you can see bubbles in the glass.

Travelers and settlers heading west in wagons often stopped here to rest or for provisions. Springfield, Missouri, served as a jumping-off point for those heading west in southern Missouri. Many wagons would stop at Kendrick House or farther south at the Ritchey House in Newtonia, Missouri, for supplies and water. At Kendrick House, pioneers could obtain goods ranging from bullets to horseshoes to guns from the Kendricks' thriving blacksmithing and gunsmithing business. They could also purchase food grown by the Kendricks and produce from their orchards. For many, Kendrick House was the most impressive house they had came into contact with in hundreds of miles. The house also served as a community sick house in the days before hospitals or doctors were common. People who were seriously ill would be brought to the Kendrick House to be cared for until they recovered or passed away. It is unknown how many people died in the house over the years, but it could be considerable, as outbreaks of diseases such malaria and tuberculosis were not uncommon.

With the Kansas state line only twenty miles away, it was only a matter of time before the hostilities in Kansas affected the Kendricks' lives. It wasn't far from here that John Brown first came to national prominence for resisting the violence of Missouri bushwhackers who set fire to abolitionist settlements at Osawatomie, Pottawattamie and Palmyra, Kansas, in 1856, the same year the Kendrick family purchased and moved into this house. Tensions indeed spilled over to southwest Missouri. Examples include the pro-abolitionist schoolteacher at Sarcoxie, Missouri, just fifteen miles from Kendrick House, who refused to heed warnings to stop preaching the virtues of the abolitionist cause to the children and found himself tarred and feathered and run out of town in 1858.

At Kendrick House, tranquility and a lifetime of labor were interrupted on July 5, 1861, when the first land battle of the war unfolded yards from their front door. Federal troops engaged Jackson at Dry Fork about eight miles north of the Kendrick farm, with fighting coming south and passing along the trail just west of the house that is now Garrison Street and is part of old Route 66. Family accounts of the battle say that troops moved south toward Spring River just yards west of the house, causing the men to drop tools and run from the fields in which they were working. During the course of the day's fighting, Kendrick House was commandeered by Union troops as a hospital, and during the days after the battle it served as a field hospital for Confederate wounded as well. Confederate general Jo Shelby also used Kendrick House as a camp on his cavalry invasion into Missouri in the fall of 1863.

Kendrick House witnessed its share of brutality from occupation by both armies and raids from bushwhackers. The Kendricks' slave woman was tortured and hanged by confederate guerrillas who believed she was hiding a Union soldier. These same guerrillas also tortured the slave woman's young daughter, Rose, and left her for dead. After the guerrilla raiders left, the family came out of their hiding place and nursed Rose back to health. Rose elected to stay at Kendrick House after the war and worked for the Kendrick family until her death at age ninety-two.

Bushwhackers came through several times, and on one occasion the farmer to the east of the Kendricks was shot sixteen times as he opened his door. The man to the west was also shot on his porch without a chance to say a word. It has been

Danger was ever present for those living in southwest Missouri during the Civil War, for one never knew if it was a friend or foe knocking at the door. *Courtesy of Alex Martin.*

speculated that the Kendricks, despite Confederate leanings, were able to avoid the brutal violence, burning and plunder of most of their neighbors due to their profession as blacksmiths and gunsmiths; their services were valuable to the troops and bushwhackers who came through, so they were more valuable alive than dead as long as they didn't provoke violence. However, William Kendrick, then sixty-five years old, came very close to death at the hands of Union soldiers in late 1864. In the course of carrying out the Federal General Order Number 11, which mandated that all men in southwest Missouri known to have Southern sympathies, or who had not taken the oath of allegiance to the Federal government, vacate the region, a Union unit came to Kendrick House looking for Joshua, known to be a Southern sympathizer.

Joshua and other men had been warned of the approaching soldiers. He decided to head to Newton County for safety. The commanding officer demanded William tell them where his son was, but the elder Kendrick was quite deaf and couldn't hear what the man had said. Frustrated, the commander drew his pistol, put it to William's head and pulled the trigger. William's wife, Elizabeth, rushed forward and placed her thumb under the hammer of the gun, preventing it from firing, saving her husband from a gunshot to the head. The commander became enraged and wildly threatened to kill the Kendricks. His men, appearing embarrassed, pulled him out of the house, with the commander yelling that he would return and kill the whole family. His men apologized to Elizabeth, saying the commander was just drunk and they wouldn't be back. The family abandoned Kendrick Place and followed Joshua to Neosho, where they stayed for the last seven months of the war.

There is also the story of Aunt Mahilia Ennis, who lived with her husband in Sennett Rankin's old log cabin. She watched troops murder her husband and then was tortured by her feet being burned by fire, leaving her crippled for the rest of her life. At another time, raiders set fire to the two-story front porch, which was wooden. After the men left, the family hitched horses to the burning porch and pulled it away from the house, avoiding damage. The family did not rebuild the porch as a reminder of what had happened.

Paranormal Science Lab conducts tours and paranormal investigations of Kendrick House, raising funds for preservation efforts for the house. Historic homes such as Kendrick House face very difficult obstacles to maintain the property or to keep the doors open to the public. Without financial support,

A Civil War Haunting

Kelly Still Harris and Lisa Livingston-Martin conduct a tour of the history of Kendrick House. *Courtesy of Paranormal Science Lab, L. Edward Martin, photographer.*

such private sites have to be innovative in fundraising, and activities that used to support preservation are no longer sustainable. Kendrick House used to host many special events and wedding parties and was a destination for tour buses, which have declined dramatically in recent years. Moreover, such historic sites face ever-increasing expenses from taxes, insurance, utilities and necessary expenses.

Victorian Carthage and Paranormal Science Lab (PSL) have worked together to raise awareness of the history of the house, as well as offer people an opportunity to experience a real-life paranormal investigation. People have traveled from all over Missouri and other states, including Kansas, Oklahoma, Iowa and Georgia, to attend Haunted History Tours and paranormal investigations. Tours focus on the history of the house and Civil War history of the area, and guests review evidence of paranormal activity documented at Kendrick House by PSL and then participate in a live investigation. All net proceeds are donated to Victorian Carthage for preservation efforts, and PSL has raised funds that have paid expenses ranging from electric bills to insurance and real estate taxes, as well as contributing to the maintenance of the property. PSL members also donate labor to Victorian Carthage to make repairs and maintenance. The

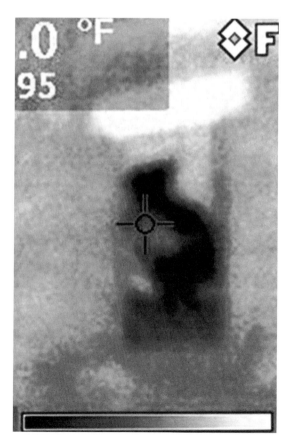

Above: Example of orbs caught at the Battle of Carthage Historic Site and Park. This is a visually interesting photo with colored orbs, which can be mistaken for paranormal activity. These are in fact particles or dust and pollen near the camera lens. *Courtesy of Paranormal Science Lab, Chelsea Copeland, photographer.*

Left: FLIR (forward looking infrared) image of parlor window at Kendrick House. An unexplained cold signature resembling the form of a woman. The coldness extends below the windowsill and is not a reflection on the glass. *Courtesy of Paranormal Science Lab, L. Edward, Martin photographer.*

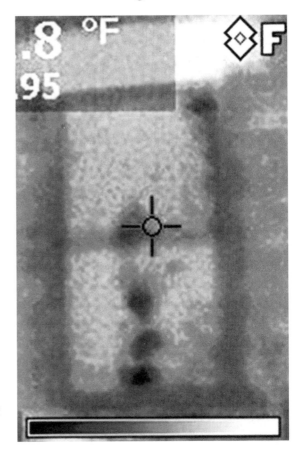

FLIR image of west parlor window at Kendrick House taken from the front yard seconds after the FLIR image of the cold signature resembling the form of a woman. *Courtesy of Paranormal Science Lab, L. Edward, Martin photographer.*

Missouri Humanities Council—which, among other things, promotes public awareness of history and works with museums and historic sites to provide educational experiences for the public—has used the Haunted History Tours offered at Kendrick Place as an example of combining the interest in history and the paranormal for fundraising at historic sites.

PSL has also been fortunate in being able to conduct extensive investigations at Kendrick House, building a large body of data that allows PSL to conduct continuing experiments based upon scientific principles, with the long-term goal of explaining the cause and nature of paranormal activity observed at Kendrick House and other sites. More information about Paranormal Science Lab's investigation methods and examples of evidence collected can be found at the PSL website: www.paranormalsciencelab.com.

WHAT CAN YOU EXPERIENCE AT KENDRICK HOUSE?

The original frame structure kitchen, which was behind the west end of the house, is long gone. The purpose of locating the kitchen outside the main structure was for safety. Cooking was done on open hearths and ovens with wood fires. Kitchen fires, often the result of catching floor-length skirts on fire, were common and one of the most common causes of injury and death to women of the mid-nineteenth century. Over time, frame additions were built and torn off the back of the original brick structure. The current addition was built in the 1980s and houses the kitchen, office space and bathrooms for Victorian Carthage. It also contains a large, long room with various artifacts found onsite from the 1800s. The room is dominated by a long, narrow dining table that is original to the house and, according to family lore, was used as the field hospital operating table. This had been merely lore until recently, when Paranormal Science Lab employed techniques used in crime scene investigations to supply corroboration of the story. As demonstrated on crime investigation television shows, law enforcement uses UV (ultraviolet) light to search for bloodstains. Paranormal Science Lab approached the table as a 149-year-old crime scene. Blood appears violet or purple under UV, no matter how long it has been there, and remnants of it remain. It is also extremely difficult to eliminate all traces of blood, even after long periods of time. Turn out the lights and turn on UV flashlights, and the ordinary, antique table takes on a vastly different appearance. At one end there are violet spots in splatter patterns, and as the UV passes down the length of the table, lines of violet illuminate the grains of the wood planks forming the tabletop. Although a bit macabre, it makes perfect sense. A military field hospital of the 1860s could be anywhere from a tent to a barn to a house commandeered, as was Kendrick House. A long table worked well, and one end would be propped up so that fluids would run off into buckets or bowls at the other end. The UV test supports the family lore handed down through 149 years that this table saw a lot of blood and thus very possibly is the operating table used by army doctors during and after the Battle of Carthage.

Interestingly, quite a few EVPs (electronic voice phenomenon) are recorded in the room where the table now sits, which ironically is in an addition that did not exist in 1861. EVPs are voices captured on audio that were not audible to those present at the time of recording. Many are at frequencies outside the range of the human voice. EVPs have been captured in the room containing the purported operating table that seem to be related to the Civil War period, including one that says "General E. Lee" and another that names Peter Hahn, a German name. The Union troops headquartered at Kendrick and working and bleeding in the field hospital were mostly German-Americans. The EVP captured says "Peter Hahn's wish" and occurs as PSL conducts a Haunted History Tour and the story of the operating table being tilted to allow fluids to flow to one end is being told. Is it possible that a Peter Hahn was present in the field hospital? Additionally, there is the coincidental fact that the name Peter Hahn is associated with the set of medical texts *A Practice of Medicine*, which were the official reference books of Union army surgeons and written by George Bacon Wood, his son-in-law. Is there a connection to his name being heard around the operating table? The sound of a hammer hitting an anvil is also heard.

Numerous EVPs have been captured at Kendrick House, and audible voices are heard at times as well. Two men have been heard in the midst of conversation. A young girl's laughter is heard, and a woman is heard calling the name Tom. Other types of evidence documented include a shadow person who has been captured on video (and still photography) appearing to attempt to interact with living persons present. Curtains move, and unexplained balls of light are seen and have been caught on video. Guests on tours have also captured photos with anomalies that are not readily explained by natural or man-made factors. Many people believe that orbs (opaque circular objects appearing in photographs) are ghosts or entities. PSL does not ascribe to that theory. Virtually all such objects appearing in a photograph are dust particles, pollen or moisture suspended in the air. These particles are actually within inches of the camera lens. When taking pictures, you can eliminate almost all such orbs by using a sun filter. People also experience cold spots that, under some theories, are an indication of paranormal activity, the assumption being that an entity manipulates available energy in the atmosphere to manifest or interact. People are touched by unseen forces or have had their hair or clothing tugged.

As you enter the parlor, you are again confronted with evidence of the Civil War. During multiple occupations, the house was commandeered for use as a headquarters. While today someone wishing not to be found may hide the car they are driving from view, during the Civil War, officers

Still image of Kendrick House kitchen area taken with camera on a tripod from the adjoining room. The field hospital operating table is in the foreground at right. *Courtesy of Paranormal Science Lab, Brian Schwartz, photographer.*

Still image of Kendrick House kitchen area from the adjoining room. The field hospital operating table is in the foreground on right. This photo was taken eight seconds after the previous photo. No one was in the kitchen, despite the shadow form visible in the doorway. *Courtesy of Paranormal Science Lab, Brian Schwartz, photographer.*

A Civil War Haunting

Marla Copeland receives some assistance in uncovering the trapdoor in the parlor at Kendrick House during a Haunted History Tour. Visitors get a glimpse of both the structure of the house, supported by huge tree trunks, and Civil War methods of hiding from danger. *Courtesy of Paranormal Science Lab, L. Edward Martin, photographer.*

would bring their horses indoors, out of sight of enemy troops. Horses were fed and boarded in the parlor. To this day, hoof prints can be seen clearly impressed into the wooden plank floor next to the fireplace. Likewise, the beautiful built-in cabinets and drawers were opened up and used as feeding troughs. On one occasion, in 1863, Confederate general Joseph Shelby, later known as the "unreconstructed Rebel" because he and his men rode to Mexico rather than surrender in 1865, fed his horses corn gathered from the Kendricks' fields. The family preserved some of the corncobs left after the troops departed, and they remain in the parlor. In the parlor, you can also view the trapdoor, fashioned by cutting lengths of the plank flooring in front of the fireplace and concealed by the rug, used by the family to conceal themselves when raiders approached. As you peer into the dark below the floor, the house's support is revealed. Two large oak tree trunks lay end to end upon a bed of rough-cut Carthage limestone and joined with a ship joint, supporting the house. There are legends of tunnels under the house leading away from the house. Although no evidence of tunnels has been discovered, in recent years volunteers at the home have been told by elderly men touring the home that they played in the tunnels as children with the Janney children.

As you proceed into the kitchen, which is in the addition to the original house, various artifacts are displayed that give insight into antebellum southwest Missouri life. Included are utensils and a set of old skeleton keys, to which no one knows what they fit. We have to return to the story of Rose, the slave girl who was attacked and left for dead when her mother was hanged in the orchard by Confederate guerrillas. As discussed earlier, the family lore said Rose was nursed back to health by the family and continued in their employment after the war until her death in her nineties. There is documentation that supports this claim. Newspaper columnist, and local resident, Arthur Grundy recounted the story of Rose in an article, "Keeper of the Keys," which was reprinted in a collection of his writings:

> *When entering Carthage, one is under the impression Spring River flows through town with a part of Carthage north of the river. The truth however is that all on the north side of the river is an entirely separate town called Kendricktown. If you ever visit our town, you will see a large weather-worn red brick house with a bit of ivy clinging to it. This is known as the Kendrick House—of an early day settler and slave owner. It was on this early day estate that a cute and winsome little girl was born into slavery and it was here [s]he lived her entire life. While it is true this little girl was born a slave—it is also true that she may have known more freedom than many of us have in our modern day lives. She was free to roam the river bottom fields as a child and the valleys of the uplands covered with wild roses, which she was very fond of, as this little girl's name was Rose. She also had the advantage of being loved by the colored folk and her white master and mistress alike. Rose grew into womanhood and there was a young man in her life by the name of George. It's not clear where George came from— perhaps he also was born on this same farm, or it may have been that he was sold to the Kendrick family while he was just a young lad. At any rate Rose and George became man and wife. It's also not clear whether they were married by a legal ceremony or if it was a common-law marriage. It seems to the writer this marriage was made in Heaven and legality would be only a minor fact of this story. These two slaves were faithful servants to their master and mistress and received kindness and love in return. It's told that when their mistress was on her death bed, Rose wept and held her in her*

Old keys hanging on the kitchen wall at Kendrick House. Perhaps these are Rose and George's keys.
Courtesy of Paranormal Science Lab, Alex Martin, photographer.

arms. A white member of this family remonstrated and begged Aunty not to die in the arms of a slave, but Aunty loved Rose and rebuked this member of her family. She said Rose had what many people in this world did not possess—"a heart of gold." God made all of us to be born and then as the years pass to grow old. This also happened to Rose and George and when they could no longer work in the fields or care for the family mansion their kindly master gave these dearly loved old slaves a feeling of importance by letting them carry the keys to the barns and house. It was their chore to lock the doors each night and unlock them each morning. They became the keepers of the keys. After the Civil War a small town grew around this stately old brick house and was named after its owner—becoming known as Kendricktown. Today this is a town filled with laughing children, flowers and gardens. The keys that Rose and George carried for so many years now hang in the weather-worn red brick house. The writer lives on the outskirts of this town and even at this extreme edge there is a feeling of safety and security. This is a feeling that could only come from above, as though God has done very much like Rose's and George's earthly master and gave them the feeling of importance of watching over our safety. It's a feeling that these two faithful old slaves are still, even though they have been in heaven these many years—KEEPERS OF THE KEYS.

Contrary to popular belief, the sentiment and affection described of the slave owner toward his slaves was not unusual in antebellum Missouri. It was not an unusual occurrence, although not universal, for slaves to be buried in family cemeteries along with family members. Behind the original kitchen, there was a sidewalk made of the same handmade bricks as are the house that led back to the slave quarters, also made of the same handmade red bricks. The original slave quarters were torn down at some point. When Victorian Carthage purchased the property, two wooden slave cabins from the Miller, Missouri area were relocated here and roofed together, so that there are actually two cabins contained in the building you see there.

You will also observe in the addition, at the east end, a fireplace with accessories that demonstrate a typical mid-nineteenth-century hearth. This was the sole cooking source for people, and as you can imagine, by cooking with a large pot over an open fire, most meals consisted of a stew or porridge. In more affluent kitchens, such as would have been in the original Kendrick House, there would have also been a stone oven fueled by a wood box and chimney for baking breads and other dishes.

As you walk through the doorway into the hallway and foyer, remember that this was the exterior wall, and a door would have been present. The staircase is a good example of the craftsmanship and level of artisans who were living on the edge of the frontier in the mid-1800s. As the house has been restored to its original form, the original trim board was uncovered. Look closely and you will see the signature of the carpenter who it is believed built the staircase, Noah Wilson, dated June 8, 1850. Jasper County census data list Noah Wilson as a carpenter living in the area. As you climb the stairs, pay attention for creaks and weak boards, and you will be amazed at how quiet and sturdy it is at more than 160 years old, creaking less than homes only a few years old.

A Civil War Haunting

On the landing, again, are items very central to life of the nineteenth century, including the spinning wheel. There is a door on the south wall over the front door. As mentioned previously, the family never rebuilt the original two-level covered porch in memory of what happened during the war, after it was burned by bushwhackers. So if you look at old photos of the house, there will be no porch. Victorian Carthage made a compromise and put the porch back but left the second level uncovered. If you go to Newtonia and see the Richie Mansion—also built by Dawson—you will see the porch as it would have appeared here. In summertime, this door to the porch served an important function. On hot, steamy nights, the door would be opened to let in air from outside in the hope that enough of a breeze would be pulled through the house to allow sleep in the bedrooms. When it was too hot and still for that, people would sleep outside on porches.

There are two large bedrooms—the master bedroom on the east end and on the west end, the children's room. Again there are items of everyday life, such as the metal bustle, which was worn under petticoats and skirts. Overhead, you will notice metal rods running the length of the room along the exterior walls. There is actually another set running between the ceiling downstairs and the floor on the second floor. These rods are not original and are not part of the structure of the house. In fact, they are a result of a form of snake oil salesman. Instead of selling snake oil medicine to cure what ails you, these salesmen cashed in on fears created by the great San Francisco earthquake of 1906. They traveled the country warning people with brick homes and other brick buildings that they needed to prepare for when "the big one" came. The selling point was that the rods would make the structure more stable and less likely to crumble in an earthquake. The reality is that it would actually make a structure slightly less stable in an earthquake than it was before installing the rods. These rods are pretty common in this part of the country. If you look at the outside of the house you will see metal stanchions, which are the pieces to which the rods are anchored and hold them in place. If you look at old brick buildings of the time, it is not uncommon to see the stanchions, which can be in shapes varying from circles to stars or anything in between.

You will see photos of some of the Kendrick family and descendants in the house, including William and Elizabeth Kendrick, who completed the house and were the first to live in it, along with their son Joshua and his family. Kendrick family descendants lived in the home for over 130 years, with generations of people being born, experiencing joy and tragedy and dying in the home. It was the site of a prosperous blacksmithing business that stretched over three generations. As such, it is not surprising that history and ethereal events coincide here.

EVPs of several voices have been captured on audio, including the woman who searches for Tom—Tom Kendrick, Joshua's son, perhaps? Or perhaps she is one of the Kendrick granddaughters searching for a Tom, lost to history. At least two other women's voices have been caught on audio, two of which are suspected to be Rose, the slave girl, and Elvira, Joshua's wife. Also documented are the voices of at least three men and, perhaps most compelling, the voice of a small child identifying herself as Carol or Carrot. Carol Jenney, great-great-granddaughter of William and Elizabeth Kendrick, died in the house in 1936, barely a day after contracting polio. Ironically, Carol's nickname was Carrot. Other indications of Carol's presence are known as well, including the overheard squeal of a child's laugh and playful interaction during EVP sessions using flashlights and balls.

PSL has also conducted investigations at the Battle of Carthage Battlefield Park. This is the spot where Major Sigel's men camped the night before the battle and the Confederate troops camped the night after the battle. The area near Carter Spring and the old cave said to be used in the Underground Railroad is very active. Outdoor investigations pose certain challenges due to being limited to battery-powered equipment, possible noise contamination and the elements.

EVPs have been captured that may be related to the Civil War battle, including multiple EVPs naming someone as Webb and warning of danger. Footsteps are often heard where there is no one walking. Investigators have had the sensation of being touched. Additionally, there has been a tendency for battery-powered instruments to experience unexplained battery drains, which is associated with paranormal activity. The theory is that the entity is manipulating the energy available in the batteries to interact.

Various types of data are collected during investigations, including atmospheric conditions, temperature, air pressure and static and fluctuating electromagnetic field readings. Data is recorded, and all photographic, video and audio data is preserved in electronic files. PSL has not as of this date made an opinion as to the nature of the phenomena described above.

Experiments are conducted during EVP sessions where PSL members conduct conversations or ask questions. High-end audio recorders, used for recording by musicians, are used to record investigations, capturing EVPs in

A Civil War Haunting

Part of the Battle of Carthage State Historic Site and Park. This area would have been filled with campfires and weary soldiers. In this part of the park, footsteps are often heard. *Courtesy of Paranormal Science Lab, Alex Martin, photographer.*

Battle of Carthage State Historic Site and Park. This is a trail leading to the bluff above the spring and the Carter House. *Courtesy of Paranormal Science Lab, L. Edward Martin, photographer.*

Above: Battle of Carthage State Historic Site and Park. This is a view from the bluff above the spring and overlooks the area both armies used as a campsite. *Courtesy of Paranormal Science Lab, L. Edward Martin, photographer.*

Left: Don't believe everything you see. This image of a man's face is simply an optical illusion created by a piece of plastic that was hanging in front of the wallpaper. PSL was able to duplicate the image multiple times. *Courtesy of Paranormal Science Lab, Eric Crinnian, photographer.*

the form of disembodied voices and other audio anomalies not audible at the time. Tools employed include various models of flashlights, referred to as "magic candles" at Kendrick House, as the term flashlight has no contextual meaning to someone from the mid-1800s. The flashlights are ordinary models purchased at major retailers. They are adjusted so that the battery connection is almost complete but so that the light is not on. The flashlights are placed on the floor, a table or other furniture. The floor is slapped with force to ensure that vibration from investigators' casual movement is not sufficient to cause the flashlight to come on. As questions are asked, any entities that may be present are requested to turn on one or more lights for an affirmative response and to leave them unlit for a negative response. Questions are asked in multiple ways so that for internal consistency, multiple responses are required, both affirmative and negative. PSL does not consider responses as an interactive exchange without consistent responses over an extended period of time, usually a minimum of a half hour, and with

Paranormal Science Lab conducts a kinetic energy experiment using a ball with colored stickers applied to track movement on video.
Courtesy of Paranormal Science Lab, L. Edward Martin, photographer.

consistent responses on multiple flashlights of multiple models. An example of such sessions is on the PSL website at the Investigations page for Kendrick House. Consistent responses involving as many as five flashlights at a time have been documented over as many as seven consecutive hours.

PSL also conducts experiments on kinetic energy, exploring theories of entities using available energy generated in the environment that are not electrical in nature. Children's balls of varying sizes, weights and materials are used and set in motion during EVP sessions, while the floors are measured for uphill and downhill slopes to determine if movement occurs that cannot be explained by the physical features of the floor and room. Colored stickers are applied to the ball so that movement can be observed more easily on video. In the children's bedroom, it is not uncommon to document movements that are contraindicated by the contours of the floor. Additionally, on several occasions, balls in a stationary position have been observed to move without contact or other natural explanation.

Lisa Livingston-Martin films with a high-speed format camera.
Courtesy of Paranormal Science Lab,
L. Edward Martin, photographer.

A Civil War Haunting

PSL uses multiple types of cameras, including wide-spectrum cameras, commonly referred to as full-spectrum cameras, which are sensitive to not only visible light, as are standard cameras, but also infrared light (utilized in night vision and security cameras) and ultraviolet light. This allows PSL to record portions of the light spectrum not visible to the human eye or standard cameras. Another type of camera used is a high-speed camera, which can record video at up to 1000 fps (frames per second). The accepted standard for recording real-time video is 30 fps, meaning that video at 1000 fps contains 33.33 times as many frames as video recorded at 30 fps. The typical television programming is replayed at 24 fps, actually slightly slower than real time. The human eye can perceive up to approximately 240 fps. This means that any movement faster than 240 fps will not be seen by the naked eye. When replaying high-speed video, the display rate is 30 fps, meaning that it takes 33.33 seconds to replay every second recorded. Every 10 seconds recorded will take 333.3 seconds (5 minutes and 33.3 seconds) to play back. The video will appear to the eye as being in slow motion, but in fact, it captures movement that cannot be caught on standard cameras. PSL has captured, at other locations, movement appearing in a general human form that was not visible to the naked eye of investigators present or the full-spectrum camera recording at 30 fps in the same area of the same room, although as of this date, this has not occurred at Kendrick House.

PSL also utilizes a FLIR (forward-looking infrared) camera, which captures thermal images, specifically contrasts in temperatures of objects in the image. While heat signatures can indicate the presence of a living creature, human, rodent or the family pet, unexplained heat signatures have to be explained. Unexplained images of a cold nature are of interest to paranormal investigators, as drops in temperature are often associated with paranormal experiences.

PSL has not as of this date made an opinion as to the nature of the phenomena described above. What is apparent, however, is that unexplained phenomena occur in various locations, including Civil War sites, which is perceived as ghosts or other forms of paranormal activity. To say that paranormal activity does not exist because it has not been fully explained simply begs the ultimate question of why these phenomena occur. After all, five hundred years ago, it was accepted fact that the Earth was flat, and a few hundred years before that, it was accepted that the Earth was the center of the universe. By investigating sites in the context of the history and lives of the people who have lived and died there, we come away with a better understanding of our history as well as the accounts of ghosts witnessed. For southwest Missouri, the Civil War was an unparalleled period of violence, sorrow and anger. As the torches burned the physical landscape, the depredations inflicted were also scorched upon the psyche of the people who lived through fires. Is it beyond the realm of possibility that such intense experiences caused those who died in those turbulent times to remain?

BIBLIOGRAPHY

Banasik, Michael E. *Duty, Honor and Country: The Civil War Experiences of Captain William P. Black, Thirty-Seventh Illinois Infantry.* Vol. 6 in *Unwritten Chapters in Civil War West of the River Series.* Iowa City, IA: Press of the Camp Pope Bookshop, 2006.

———. *Missouri in 1861: The Civil War Letters of Franc Bangs Wilkie.* Iowa City, IA: Press of the Camp Pope Bookshop, 2001.

Belk, Colleen. *Jasper County, Missouri Tombstones and Civil War Data.* Huntsville, AR: Century Enterprises, 1990.

Bolivar Weekly Courier [Bolivar, MO], April 14, 1860.

Brink-McDonough & Co. *An Illustrated Historical Atlas Map of Jasper County, Missouri.* Philadelphia, 1876.

Brophy, Patrick. *Found No Bushwackers: The 1864 Diary of Sgt. James P. Mallery, Company A, Third Wisconsin Cavalry Stationed at Balltown, Missouri.* Nevada, MO: Vernon County Historical Society, 1988.

———. *Knights of the Bush and Others [Rebels and Yankees].* Nevada, MO: Vernon County Historical Society, 2005.

Brownlee, Richard S. *Gray Ghosts of the Confederacy: Guerilla Warfare in the West, 1861–1865.* First Edition. Baton Rouge: Louisiana State University Press, 1958.

Cottrell, Steve. *The Battle of Carthage and Carthage in the Civil War.* Carthage, MO: City of Carthage, 1990.

————. *Haunted Ozarks Battlefields: Civil War Ghost Stories and Brief Battle Histories*. First Pelican Edition. Gretna, LA: Pelican Publishing Co., 2010.

Cunningham, Frank. *General Stand Watie's Confederate Indians*. Norman: University of Oklahoma Press, 1998.

1860 Jasper County Slave Census. Carthage: Jasper County, Missouri Records Center Collection.

Gilbert, Joan. *Missouri Ghosts: Spirits, Haunts and Related Lore…* Columbia, MO: Pebble Publishing, 1997.

Gilmore, Donald L. *Civil War on the Missouri-Kansas Border*. Gretna, LA: Pelican Publishing Company, Inc., 2006.

Greer, Lillie Johnson. *Through the Years, A History of Peace Church Cemetery: 104 Years/Sherwood Cemetery 100 Years in Galena Township*. N.p., 1961.

Grundy, Arthur. *Art's Scrapbook: Reminisces Over the Years with Arthur Grundy*. Collected works from "Over the Ozarks" column of the *Springfield [MO] Daily News*. Illustrations by Susie Schaeffer. N.p., 1970.

Hale, Donald R. *They Called Him Bloody Bill: The Life of William Anderson Missouri Guerilla, The Missouri Badman Who Taught Jesse James Outlawry*. Clinton, MO: The Printery, 1975.

————. *We Rode with Quantrill: Quantrill and the Guerrilla War as Told by the Men Who Were with Him, With a True Sketch of Quantrill's Life*. Clinton, MO: The Printery, 1975.

Hinds, Bob. *Ozark Pioneers: Their Trials and Triumphs*. Seventh Printing. Willow Springs, MO: Bob Hinds Books, 2002.

Hinze, David C. *The Battle of Carthage: Border War in Southwest Missouri July 5, 1861*. First Pelican Printing. Gretna, LA: Pelican Publishing Co., Inc., 2004.

James, Larry A. *Pioneers of the Six Bulls: The Newton County, Missouri Saga*. Neosho, MO: Newton County Historical Publications, 1981.

Johnson, Robert Underwood, and Clarence Clough Buel, eds. *Battles and Leaders of the Civil War: Being for the Most Part Contributions of Union and Confederate Officers*. Vol. 1. Boston: Houghton, Mifflin and Co., 1889.

Livingston, John C., Jr. *Such a Foe as Livingston: The Campaign of Confederate Major Thomas R. Livingston's First Missouri Cavalry Battalion of Southwest Missouri*. Wyandotte, OK: Gregath Publishing Company, 2004.

Missouri State Highway Patrol. Introduction to Missouri Historical Society Press edition of *Marshall, Missouri: WPA Guide to the "Show Me" State*, by Walter A. Schroeder and Howard W. Schroeder. New York: Duell, Sloan and Pearce, 1941. Reprint, St. Louis: Missouri Historical Society Press, 1998.

Monks, William. *A History of Southern Missouri and Northern Arkansas, Being an Account of the Early Settlements, the Civil War, the Ku-Klux, and Times of Peace.* West Plains, MO: West Plains Journal Co., 1907.

Musick, John R. *Stories of Missouri.* New York: American Book Company, 1897.

O'Donnell, Billy, and Karen Glines. *Painting Missouri: The Counties en Plein Air.* Columbia: University of Missouri Press, 2008.

Offutt, Jason. *Haunted Missouri: A Ghostly Guide to the Show-Me State's Most Spirited Spots.* First Edition. Kirksville, MO: Truman State University Press, 2007.

Randolph, Vance. *Ozark Ghost Stories: Gruesome and Humorous Tales of the Supernatural in the Backwoods of South.* Photo-facsimile edition of 1944 Haldeman-Julius Publications edition. Forrest City, AR: Marshall Vance, 1982.

————. *Ozark Magic and Folklore.* New York: Dover Publications, 1964.

Rossiter, Phyllis. *A Living History of the Ozarks.* N.p., n.d.

Schrantz, Ward L. *Jasper County, Missouri, in the Civil War.* Reprint. Originally published 1923. Carthage, MO: Carthage, Missouri Kiwanis Club, 2010.

Shoemaker, Floyd Calvin. *Missouri and Missourians: Land of Contrasts and People of Achievements.* Vol. 1. Chicago, 1943.

Snead, T.L. *The Fight for Missouri, from the Election of Lincoln to the Death of Lyon.* Astor Place, NY: J.J. Little Co., 1886.

Steele, Phillip W., and Steve Cottrell. *Civil War in the Ozarks.* Sixth Printing. Gretna, LA: Pelican Publishing Co., 2003.

Stephens, Mrs. Ann S. *Pictorial History of the War for the Union.* Cincinnati, OH: James R. Hawley Publisher, 1863.

Stevens, Walter Barlow. *Missouri the Center State: 1821–1915.* 3 vols. Chicago: S.J. Clarke Publishing Co., 1915.

Sturges, Judge J.A. *A History of McDonald County, Missouri.* N.p., 1897. Reprinted by McDonald County Public Library, Pineville, MO, 2003, free download pdf form, available at www.librarymail.org/genehist/sturgesbookv2_2.pdf.

Tremeear, Janice. *Missouri's Haunted Route 66: Ghosts Along the Mother Road.* Charleston, SC: The History Press, 2010.

VanGilder, Marvin L. *Jasper County: The First Two Hundred Years.* Rich Hill, MO: Bell Books, 1995.

Wood, Larry. *The Civil War on the Lower Kansas-Missouri Border*. Second Edition. Joplin, MO: Hickory Press, 2003.

———. *Other Noted Guerrillas of the Civil War in Missouri*. Joplin, MO: Hickory Press, 2007.

Woodruff, W.E. *With the Light Guns in '61–'65: Reminiscences of Eleven Arkansas, Missouri and Texas Light Batteries, in the Civil War*. Little Rock, AR: Central Printing Co., 1903.

WEBSITES

Community in Conflict: The Impact of the Civil War in the Ozarks: Springfield/Greene County Library and other archives database. www.ozarkscivilwar.org/archives/1140.

Cottey College. www.cottey.edu.

Cottey College Cotteyphile. cotteyphile.com.

Midwest Archeological Center, National Park Service, U.S. Department of the Interior. www.cr.nps.gov/mwac/wicr_peri/wilsons_creek.htm.

Missouri Humanities Council. www.mohumanities.org/news-updates/missouri-passages/november-2010-vol-7-no-9/exploring-a-haunted-history.

Missouri Secretary of State, Missouri Digital Heritage. www.sos.mo.gov/mdh.

National Park Service, U.S. Department of the Interior, Military Medicine at Wilson's Creek. www.nps.gov/wicr/historyculture/civil-war-medicine.htm.

Paranormal Science Lab. www.paranormalsciencelab.com.

Springfield-Greene County, Missouri online local history collection. thelibrary.springfield.missouri.org/lochist.

ABOUT THE AUTHOR

L isa Livingston-Martin is a lifelong resident of southwest Missouri, living in Webb City, Missouri, with her husband and three sons. Lisa is an attorney and has had a longtime passion for history. Lisa is also a co-team leader of Paranormal Science Lab, which focuses on paranormal research at historic sites.

Lisa Livingston-Martin at Civil War monument in National Cemetery Number 2, Baxter Springs, Kansas. *Courtesy of L. Edward Martin.*

Visit us at
www.historypress.net